OWN YO

THE FABIAN SERIES

Series Editor Ben Pimlott

Forthcoming titles

OWN YOUR OWN
Social Ownership Examined

Oonagh McDonald

UNWIN
PAPERBACKS

LONDON SYDNEY WELLINGTON

First published in paperback by Unwin Paperbacks, an imprint of Unwin Hyman Limited, in 1989

Unwin Hyman Limited
15–17 Broadwick Street
London W1V 1FP

Allen & Unwin Australia Pty Ltd
8 Napier Street, North Sydney, NSW 2060, Australia

Allen & Unwin New Zealand Pty Ltd with the Port Nicholson Press
Compusales Building, 75 Ghuznee Street, Wellington, New Zealand

---

British Library Cataloguing in Publication Data

McDonald, Ooonagh
   Own your own: social ownership examined.
—(Fabian series).
1. Great Britain. Public sector.
Privatisation
I. Title   II. Series
354.4107'2
ISBN 0 09 182383 8

Typeset in 10 on 11 point Garamond
by Saxon Printing Ltd, Derby.
Printed and bound in Great Britain by
Cox & Wyman Ltd, Reading

Contents

General Editor's Preface

The Fabian Research Unit series of short books has been launched in the belief that the policies of the Thatcher administration are dangerous and immoral; that they are very far from inevitable; but that they are likely to continue until clear alternatives are known and understood.

The second – and major – purpose is to develop a genuine radicalism, based on principles of equality, fairness and collective responsibility. The studies are 'Fabian' in the sense of an interest in practicality: they will be concerned with the political and administrative means of achieving goals. They will take no refuge in cautious moderation, but seek instead a rational extremism, exploring the limits of possible progress.

The series is connected to no party. Each study – by a distinguished political, academic or journalistic author – is a personal contribution. It does not necessarily express the views of the Fabian Research Unit or of the Fabian Society with which the Unit is associated.

Ben Pimlott
Director
Fabian Research Unit

Chapter 1
Selling the Family Silver

For forty years, the Labour Party, and perhaps most of the British public, took the state ownership of basic industries and the public utilities for granted. In 1979, the Conservatives were elected with a manifesto commitment to sell off the aerospace and shipbuilding industries, together with the companies owned by the National Enterprise Board, which was to be disbanded. But Mrs Thatcher later decided to sell off state owned assets, to privatize them. The Labour Party and the trade unions have opposed each privatization measure since then with no success and with only lukewarm support at best from the public. The Prime Minister faced some opposition from within her own ranks, typified in Lord Stockton's famous accusation that she was selling off the family silver. The objection was to the price at which the assets were sold, not to the principle of denationalization.

The process of privatization has forced socialists to reconsider the reasons for their adherence to public ownership. The family silver may have been sold off cheaply, but buying it back will be very expensive. That very fact should make socialists ask themselves why they wanted to own certain industries in the first place. The Labour Party's commitment to public ownership is thought to be contained in Clause 4 of its constitution, 'To secure for the workers by hand or by brain the full fruits of their industry and the most equitable distribution thereof that may be possible upon the basis of the common ownership of the means of production, distribution and exchange, and the best obtainable system of popular administration and control of each industry or service.' It has just been assumed that it means more state ownership, although 'common ownership' is not identical with 'state ownership'. Little thought has been given to the principles contained in Clause 4 or to how these can best be applied to society now. The meaning and application of Clause 4 has to be reconsidered as a result of privatization. That is the theme of this book. The possible privatization of services, such as health and education, predominantly provided collectively, is not under consideration here, since these are generally regarded as non-profit-making concerns, which should be largely a matter of public sector provision.

The issue of social ownership has centred on profit-making, commodity-producing enterprises.

The sheer scale of privatization is daunting. To date, sixteen major public companies, employing 650,000 people and accounting for 40 per cent of the state sector, have been wholly or partially privatized; total net receipts to date, excluding British Airport Authorities and British Petroleum (BP), amount to £17.8 billion. The net Exchequer receipts from the sale of shares in the major shareholdings were £4.361 billion from British Telecom in 1984, £7.731 billion from British Gas in November 1986, and £1.036 billion from Rolls Royce in April 1987.

Receipts to come were expected to amount to £40 billion immediately after the election in June 1987, when it was thought that BP would raise over £7 billion, the water authorities, £8 billion and the electricity supply industry, £18 billion. Following the October 1987 stock market crash, no one can be certain.

Privatization was a little-noticed commitment in the 1979 Conservative election manifesto, arising out of impatience with the inefficiencies of nationalized industries and the problems of finding an effective system for managing them. The programme really took off with the sale of British Telecom in November 1984. Privatization then became a useful source of extra revenue, and a means of discouraging voters, since so many new shareholders would stand to lose financially from re-nationalization, from supporting any party which appeared to be committed to that. Although this objective is rarely expressed, privatization is probably seen by the Government as another means of disciplining the power of public sector trade unions. Ministers, of course, justified it in quite different terms. Privatization would lead to better management, since it would free the companies from Whitehall bureaucratic control; and companies would be more efficient, because they would be directly accountable to private investors and would no longer be obliged to meet arbitrary and changing objectives laid down by Government. The Government also used privatization to promote wider share ownership, or 'popular capitalism'. Employees were encouraged to become shareholders in the concerns they worked for by means of preferential equity offerings, and thus to identify more closely with the company.

The ground has shifted from time to time. The first concern was with liberalization, as shown by the 1980 Transport Act, which deregulated express coaching, and in the 1981 Telecommunications Act and the 1983 Energy Act. After that, the main objective became the transfer of ownership, with competition as the overriding aim, as John Moore, then Financial Secretary to the Treasury, said in

November 1983. These words were never supported by actions. By 1985, the Government made it clear that it would continue to privatize natural monopolies where 'competition does not make business or economic sense'.

This marks a change in Government policy. In the November 1983 speech, John Moore insisted that the aim was to secure real efficiency gains through the promotion of competition, when he said,

> Activities such as electricity generation, the production and marketing of gas, coal production and sale, telecommunications ... bus transport, sewerage treatment and disposal are in no sense natural monopolies. The monopolies in these areas were created [not natural] and it is by no means self-evident that they are necessary or even beneficial.
>
> The primary objective of the Government's privatisation programme is to reduce the power of monopolises and to encourage competition. ... No state monopoly is sacrosanct. We intend through competition and privatisation to open up the State sector to the stimulus of competition and reverse the creeping bureaucratisation of the last thirty-five years ... The long-term success of the privatisation programme will stand or fall by the extent to which it maximises competition. If competition cannot be achieved, an historic opportunity will have been lost.

John Moore had conveniently forgotten his words two years later. In a speech made in July 1985, shortly after the announcement of the sale of British Gas as a private monopoly, he said,

> Privatisation has proved of such major benefit over the last five years, we have decided it right to extend it progressively to the so-called 'natural monopolies'. These are the monopolies where economies of scale and barriers to entry are such that it would be artificial, wasteful or impractical to break them up. The cheapest means of producing or supplying a commodity in these circumstances may well be a natural monopoly. We believe that it is possible to privatise natural monopolies in such a way that their customers, their employees and the economy as a whole will all benefit.

But, however much the grounds for proclaiming the virtues of privatization have changed, the Government has made such large claims and has invested so much political capital in it that its failure to deliver all the economic goods will be enough to call the whole programme into question. The Government has certainly been so anxious to sell off the large monopoly utilities that it has made no effort to curb their market dominance and subject them to competitive disciplines. They merely became private monopolies, and arguably less accountable. Ministers dismissed such criticisms from their own backbenchers and the Opposition alike. British Telecom is a notorious example of that. It may account for the public's changing attitude to privatization.

Attitudes to privatization and more nationalization have changed considerably over the past eight years, and it is worth charting the changes. By the autumn of 1979, support for more public ownership (the name – contrary to claims made by some Labour Party politicians makes little difference, and, at any rate, the term 'public ownership' has been used since the post-war Labour Governments) had fallen from 31 per cent in the autumn of 1974 to 20 per cent and hit a low of 18 per cent in the autumn of 1981. It then rose to 28 per cent in the spring of 1987, but did little to help Labour in the General Election campaign. At the same time, public support for de-nationalization had fallen to 32 per cent, though here the term does make a difference. If the question concerns 'privatization', then 7 per cent more respondents favour it – 39 per cent in 1987. This is because the Conservatives identify more strongly when the programme is described as privatization, recognising it as an important part of the Conservative Government's programme.

A poll commissioned by the *Sunday Times* and conducted by MORI in October, and published in November 1987, showed growing opposition to the Government's future privatization plans. Selling off the water authorities to private shareholders arouses the greatest opposition, up from 59 per cent to 64 per cent between June and October, reflecting the fact that water is seen as the most fundamental service. Privatizing the electricity supply is almost as strongly opposed, 61 per cent compared with 56 per cent at the time of the election. Most people believe that it would mean a worse service to consumers; 53 per cent in the case of the water authorities and 52 per cent for electricity supply. Experience with British Telecom obviously colours their attitudes. Hardly anyone believes that the service has improved, only 6 per cent, compared with the 45 per cent who believe that the service has deteriorated.

It is much more difficult to see what that means for the Government's privatization programme and for Labour's plans. It would be unwise to read too much into the apparent disenchantment with it. Privatization has never commanded majority support, and the opinion poll evidence shows that it has been falling since 1981. There were signs of more opposition to the sale of British Gas than to British Telecom, yet the public still bought the shares. The effects of expensive publicity for each privatization must be taken into account, together with the inducements to individual shareholders to buy and keep the shares, and the price at which they are sold. The public, whatever misgivings they may claim to have, do recognize a bargain basement sale when they see one, and will, not surprisingly, make sure they get in on the act.

The effects of the stock market crash on future privatizations, after the BP debacle, are much more difficult to determine. The BP privatization was the last in the 1987–8 fiscal year, in which the Government has also benefited from the sale of Rolls Royce plc, Royal Ordnance, now owned by British Aerospace plc, the second call on British Gas plc and the first tranche of BAA plc, formerly the British Airports Authority. The Government will be free to sell its remaining 49.9 per cent in British Telecom after April 1989, but apparently no firm decision has yet been taken about this. It had set an annual target of £5 billion from privatization over the next four years.

Until the BP sale, privatization had netted £4 billion. The BP sale brought in $5.4 billion, well below the target of over £7 billion, with a buy-back of 39 million of the partly paid shares at a cost of £27 million. It also enabled the Kuwait Investment Office to gain enough shares to demand a seat on the Board. In the 1988–9 financial year, the Government expects £1.6 billion from the third tranche of British Gas in April, £720 million from the second tranche of BAA in May and the second instalment of BP in August was expected to bring in large proceeds, although of course since the crash no one can be sure that far ahead just how much the proceeds of privatization will be.

Quite apart from this, many City analysts believe that continuing controversy over British Telecom's performance and growing doubts about the difficulties and time taken over preparing legislation to sell off the electricity supply industry have put the privatization programme under pressure. The power industry flotation, the largest ever, is not expected until 1990 at any rate. Other sales will include British Steel, the Rover Group plc and possibly British Coal, but these are not expected until the 1990s. But whatever happens to the Government's privatization programme the fact remains that extensive sell-offs have already taken place, and at least some more must be expected. The Labour Party should consider its future policy on the assumption that very little industry or the utilities will be left in public ownership by 1991, and that many small investors will retain their shareholdings, if only because of the costs involved in selling them.

Increased efficiency and productivity, higher profits and a sharper response to the market are the benefits privatization is supposed to bring in its train. Some companies, such as Cable and Wireless, may have benefited. Others have engaged in development which might have been difficult under state ownership, such as Associated British Ports' development of 2,000 acres previously left idle, and British

Aerospace has bought Sperry Gyroscope (UK) to enter the US executive jet market, though they need not have been hindered by it.

Other evidence does little to support the ministers' case. The Institute of Fiscal Study's analysis of the first stage of the privatization of the National Bus Company, the deregulation of express coaching routes by ending the monopoly of National Express, a subsidiary of the publicly owned National Bus Company, shows that even that step was not entirely satisfactory. Their reassessment of coach deregulation suggested that 'the introduction of competition in sectors formerly the preserve of state monopolies is worthwhile, but making competition work requires more than simply removing the statutes that prohibit it ... effective competition requires an effective competition policy' (S. M. Jaffer and D. J. Thompson, *Deregulating Express Coaches: A Reassessment*, Institute of Fiscal Studies). The Government has shown very little interest in competition policy at any time during the past eight years. The consumer pays the price for their unwillingness to act.

Transferring monopoly suppliers to private ownership may encourage them to maximize profits, but it gives little incentive to increase efficiency, cut costs or improve the quality of service to customers. Competition is supposed to achieve these goals. No effort has been made to provide the main monopoly suppliers with any real competition, with obvious effects on consumers. British Telecom has taken steps to reorganize, speed up the modernization of its network and cut waiting lists for telephones. But all of these changes were under way in 1981, as a response to the liberalization of the telecommunications market. British Telecom faces some competition in its core business of network transmission, but it is limited to one operator, Mercury. This will make no difference to residential consumers.

The individual consumer has had to face sharp price rises, whilst the business consumer has been protected by the way in which the price rise formula RPI minus 3 has been applied. Long delays in fault repairs, new charges for maintenance services and out-of-order telephone kiosks have all served to undermine the Government's view that efficiency has been improved, as opposed to profitability. British Telecom's research and development programme has been cut back. The method of financing has been changed. It is no longer financed nationally, but by individual sponsoring divisions of the company, which means that the only research likely to be sponsored is that which has an identifiable, relatively short-term return. The company's policy of purchasing 95 per cent of its requirements within the United Kingdom has been modified. The purchase of a digital telephone exchange, System Y, from Ericsson of Sweden marks a significant change in policy.

The decline in the standard of services in British Telecom is a direct consequence of the Government's attitude to privatization. But the emphasis on the 'virtues of denationalisation over, and even at the expense of, the promotion of competition ... is not supported by empirical evidence on the relative performance of public and private enterprise. This stresses the role of competition and supports scepticism about the privatisation outside a competitive environment (J. Kay and D. Thompson, 'Privatisation', *Economic Journal*, Vol. 96, March 1986, pp. 18–32).

The more important objective from the point of view of this discussion is the Government's use of denationalization to achieve wider share ownership. It is only one of the methods used, which include incentives for employee share ownership, employee option ownership, discretionary employee and management share options, together with personal equity plans, all designed to reverse the decline in direct share ownership by individuals that took place in the 1960s and 1970s. It is the most effective means of promoting share ownership, partly because of the hard sell, and partly because the shares were set at attractive prices (some would say deliberately undersold).

The position in 1979 was that the number of individuals directly owning shares fell from just over 7 per cent in 1958 to 4.5 per cent. By 1983, the proportion of adults owning shares had risen to 5 per cent, but, by 1987, 8.5 million, one in five adults, almost 20 per cent, owned shares (according to a joint Treasury/Stock Exchange survey, carried out by NOP in February 1987). This change was due to the huge privatizations, such as British Gas and British Telecom. Just over two million individuals bought shares in British Telecom, in addition to employee shareholders. Some estimates suggest that this flotation alone attracted one million shareholders to the stock market, who had never owned shares before.

Once having entered the market, some of the first-time share buyers continued to buy. Although, for example, the Government's Personal Equity Plan attracted only 165,000 investors by September 1987, despite the dramatically rising market in the first seven months of that year, one building society Personal Equity Plan provider gave an interesting profile of those who had bought shares under the scheme. A survey by the Bradford and Bingley Building Society carried out in July and August 1987 showed that 54 per cent of its sales came from people who had never invested in the stock market, with the rate of purchases amongst semi-skilled and skilled workers almost twice that of professional people. Its typical first-time investor under PEP was a 57-year-old northern housewife, who put in £1,200 from her building society account. Since the stock market crash, the funds have been flowing into the building societies, and the typical buyer of the above survey may not be so easy to find.

Other features of the increase in the number of shareholders are much as one might expect, given the North-South divide. A quarter of the shareholders are located in the South-East and East Anglia, followed by 15.6 per cent in the Midlands, followed by 10.3 per cent in the North-West, and 9 per cent in Yorks/Humber. Only 4.2 per cent of the shares are owned by those living in the North.

There is a good deal of evidence to suggest that the new shareholders do not retain their shares. The most outstanding case in which this happened was that of Amersham International. There were 263,000 applications for shares and 63,760 successful applications, but by 1986 there were only 6,572 shareholders, just over 10 per cent of the successful applicants. Even with British Telecom, the number of individual shareholders has already fallen to 1.4 million (March 1987) and may have fallen still further since then, as the three-year period ended in December 1987 in which the original share-holders, who chose to have the one-in-ten script issue as a loyalty perk, may have decided to sell. At the same time, the proportion of shares held by pension funds had increased from 3.2 per cent in May 1985 to 16.2 per cent in March 1987, whilst the proportion of shares held by individuals fell from 13.7 per cent in May 1985 to 11.5 per cent in March 1987 (source: British Telecom plc, Annual Reports). The same pattern has been repeated in the other major privatizations. British Gas attracted the most individual shareholders, 4.5 million in December 1986. By April 1987, the number had fallen by 31 per cent, so that they only control 37 per cent of the shares. British Airways was sold in February 1987 and there were 1.2 million successful individuals, of whom almost half a million had sold their shares by May. In each case, although the individual shareholders form a very high proportion of the total number of shareholders, they control only a small proportion of the shares, 37 per cent in the case of British Gas and 16 per cent in the case of British Airways (source: *Labour Research*, September 1987).

The Government's own figures concentrate on the increased number of individual shareholders, since that is the most telling figure from their point of view. It has to be seen against the background of the changes in ownership of the stock market. Between 1963 and 1981, the proportion of the stock market directly owned by individuals fell from from 54 per cent to 28 per cent, and continues to fall. Shares are increasingly held by institutional shareholders – insurance companies, pension funds, investment and unit trusts, in a pattern which is repeated in other advanced industrial countries. The proportion of wealth held in shares had declined sharply in the 1970s. Further, although the value of shares owned by individuals is increasing, it is not increasing as rapidly as the value of shares owned by the financial institutions.

If the Government wanted to achieve the goal of more people owning shares, then this has certainly been achieved. It is the result of a carefully balanced package: selling privatization shares to 'Sid', schemes to encourage the sale of shares to employees, share option schemes for management and strengthening the share base through personal equity plans. This part of the plan has been successful. Little else has. In that sense, privatization has not been a radical change. The way in which privatization has been organized shows that it was never part of the Government's purpose that privatized industries should be more accountable to shareholders, still less to the consumer. The number of passive shareholders has increased, and those who have wanted to take a more active interest in the company, such as British Gas shareholders or Trustee Savings Bank shareholders (although that was not, strictly speaking, a privatization), have found that the opportunities provided by the annual meeting to influence decisions have been either limited or ineffective or both.

Privatization has not given power to shareholders, or extended industrial democracy at work, since individual employees have not been allowed to use their combined shares as a block vote. Nor has the increase in the number of shareholders made any contribution to the distribution of wealth. Increasing the number of shareholders has not been a radical step for this Government, but selling council houses has. This will substantially increase the wealth held by individuals, if not for this generation then for the next.

Share ownership has contributed nothing to a fairer distribution of wealth. This can be seen from the Inland Revenue's estimates of the distribution of personal wealth. This is

> very much concentrated amongst the top 10 per cent of wealth holders. In 1984, this group accounted for 52 per cent of total personal marketable wealth and the top 1 per cent is slightly over one fifth; the lower half held only 7 per cent ... but when compared to 1966 and the 1970s it represents a sizeable reduction in equality. For instance in 1966 the top 1 per cent held one third of the total, the top 19 per cent had 69 per cent and the lower half only 3 per cent. Since 1980 the distribution has changed little and it appears the trend towards less inequality has halted. (T.Stark, *Income and Wealth in the 1980s*, Fabian Society, 1987)

The Inland Revenue statistics for 1987 reveal an even more

interesting story. Table 7.5 shows that the trend towards greater equality in marketable wealth was quite marked in the 1970s. The top 10 per cent owned 65 per cent of this wealth in 1971, 60 per cent in 1976, and this dropped to 54 per cent in 1981, dipped again in the early 1980s, but rose from 52 per cent in 1984 to 54 per cent again in 1985, after the first major privatization. The trend, in other words, to less inequality has not just been halted but seems to have been reversed. More people may own shares, but so far ownership of company shares by individuals is still highly concentrated in the hands of very wealthy individuals. The richest 1 per cent of the population own over half the company shares, and nearly two-thirds of the land. The richest 5 per cent own 80 per cent of the shares and 86 per cent of the land, according to the latest available figures. The very wealthy own the most company shares. It also makes them richer than any other kind of asset. The real value of these assets has increased more than any other asset type since 1975, and especially since 1979. Between 1979 and 1986 company share prices more than doubled. House prices rose on average by 90 per cent up to 1985, and agricultural land by 7 per cent (ibid., p. 41).

So in spite of all the hullabaloo over wider share ownership, the rich have become richer and continue to own most of the shares. Ownership for most people is very thinly spread. A survey conducted for the Trustee Savings Bank by Dewe Rogerson in 1986 shows that 59 per cent held shares in only one company and 18 per cent held shares in four or more companies. More recently, the *Financial Times* reported that most people (60 per cent) own shares in just one company, that being the company for which they work.

Privatization, as we have seen, raised over £17 billion in additional revenue for the Government (although, curiously, it is counted as negative public expenditure in the Government's accounts, in accordance with IMF guidelines). This money has been used to finance tax cuts since 1979. The Government has, however, taken care to ensure that the tax cuts are unequally distributed as well. According to one recent Parliamentary answer, since 1979 tax-payers have paid £11.73 billion less in income tax as a result of tax changes. Nearly three-fifths went to those earning £15,000 a year or more. By 1988, this group constituted 22.3 per cent of those eligible to pay tax. By the end of the end of the 1988-9 tax year, those earning over £70,000 are estimated to be £19,100 better off because of the tax system changes. By comparison, those earning under £5,000 and £10,000 benefited to the tune of £90 and £250 respectively. (source: *Financial Times*, 28 Jan. 1988).This is just one way in which the unequal distribution of the tax changes since 1979 may be estimated.

On any analysis, however, and especially if national insurance contributions are included in the calculation, the distribution of tax cuts has been quite inequitable. For anyone on below average earnings, the proportion of income taken in tax and national insurance contributions has increased and for those above average income it has decreased.

The privatization programme has not been as radical as the Government would have us believe. At the 1986 Conservative Party conference, the Party adopted the slogan 'Power to the People' and the Prime Minister talked about shifting the balance of wealth and power towards working people and their families. Nothing of the sort has happened.

This is the situation Labour faces: gross inequality, restrictions on workers' power, and a deteriorating service to consumers. But public ownership has been dismantled with little resistance from the public. Loss of ownership of public utilities plainly meant little to people who never felt that they owned the gas or electricity services in the first place, or had any real influence over the standard of service offered. But to abandon state ownership would be to set aside the distinguishing feature of socialism in the eyes of many socialists. It would mean giving up part of the very constitution of the Labour Party.

Just because this is such a strong element in current socialist thought, it is worth examining how Clause 4 came to be part of the Party's constitution, and how and why it found its expression in the nationalization programme of the post-war Labour Governments.

Chapter 2
Social Ownership and the Labour Party

The Labour Party is identified with state ownership of industry in the minds of the public. This has been reinforced by the determined, but ineffective, opposition of the Labour Party and the trade unions to privatization, arising out of their long-standing commitment to the view that the basic utilities and industries essential to the nation's security should be publicly owned.

The trade unions campaigned against the major privatization measures, partly out of this commitment and partly to protect the interests of their membership. Trade union membership in state-owned industries is higher than in comparable private companies. Proper consultation procedures had been established in most nationalized industries, enabling the trade unions to have some influence over policy and conditions of employment. Understandably enough, they feared that privatization would lead to a change to an abrasive management style, favoured by the Government, and a worsening of the conditions of employment, including pay, for their members. But the campaigns failed to capture public support. The Government, with its overwhelming Parliamentary majority, carried its legislation through Parliament, and has the necessary majority to secure the privatization of water, electricity, steel and coal by 1992, should it wish to do so.

There are signs of weakening trade union opposition to privatization, as with the statement of the Iron and Steel Trades Confederation that it would not oppose the selling off of British Steel. The Labour Party's attitude has slowly changed, as Party conference has moved from re-nationalization without compensation to the acceptance of the NEC statement on social ownership to Party conference in 1986, which explored a variety of forms of social ownership. The Party should now reconsider the nature of its commitment to public ownership. This can best be done by re-examining Clause 4 and its implementation by the post-war Labour Governments of 1945–51.

Clause 4 was adopted as part of the Party's constitution in 1918, when the Labour Party as we now know it came into being, replacing the Labour Representation Committee, established in 1900. Prior to that, the Labour Party was a federation of trade unions and socialist societies, without individual membership. The structure of the Party and its 'programme' were established in 1918. Together with Clause 5, Clause 4 was intended as a statement of the Party's socialist objectives.

Two versions of Clause 4 were considered by the National Executive Committee; the first 'to secure for the producers by hand and by brain the full fruits of their industry by the common ownership of all monopolies and essential raw materials'. The second went wider: 'To secure for the producers by hand or brain the full fruits of their industry and the most equitable thereof that may be possible upon the basis of common ownership of the means of production and the best obtainable system of popular administration of each industry or service'. Both were considered by the National Executive Committee, but there is no record of why the second version, almost certainly Sidney Webb's, was chosen instead of the first, almost certainly Arthur Henderson's. Both versions were designed to exclude syndicalism. Arthur Henderson, whose visit to Russia had convinced him of the necessity of finding a bulwark against Bolshevism, described the desire there to adopt a 'form of syndicalism', to place 'directors and managers in a subordinate position and the supreme control in the hands of the work-people themselves' and to warn that 'if the experiment is tried, it can only have results that will be a disaster to the whole concern' (quoted by Ross McKibben, *The Evolution of the Labour Party, 1910–24*, Oxford University Press, 1974, p. 92). Sidney Webb's version was chosen, partly because Henderson apparently did not care which version was chosen.

Sidney Webb's choice of words was more deliberate. He believed that this approach would appeal to the middle classes, to whom both the Fabians and the Guild Socialists, led by G. D. Cole, thought the war had revealed where their real interests lay. He thought that his version of Clause 4 made the Party's aims clearly socialist. In an article in the *Observer* on 21 October 1917, he wrote that the 'Labour Party of the future ... is to be a Party of the producers, whether manual workers or brain workers, associated against the private owners of land and capital as such. Its policy of "common ownership" brings it decidedly under the designation of socialist' (quoted by L. Radice in *Beatrice and Sidney Webb, Fabian Socialists*, London, 1984, p. 212).

His socialism was, however, pragmatic. But it is worth recording his words about Clause 4.

> This declaration of the Labour Party leaves it open to choose from time to time whatever forms of common ownership from the co-operative store to the nationalised railway and whatever forms of popular administration and control of industry, from national guild to ministries of employment, and municipal management may, *in particular cases* [Sidney Webb's italics] commend themselves. (ibid., p. 214).

The term 'national guilds' refers to Cole's work, *Guild Socialism Restated*, in which he rejected nationalization both as a method and as an aim. 'Nationalisation, carried out under capitalism, does not really abolish private ownership, but only changes the private property claim from a varying claim on the profits of a particular industry to a fixed claim on the national resources as a whole', without any immediate benefit to the workers (p. 21).

The alternative was to place the control of industry in the hands of the workers of each factory and industry organized in comprehensive industrial unions called 'guilds'. The whole population would be organized through co-operative retail societies and local government bodies to articulate the needs of the consumers. Industrial production would be carried on for use as directed by consumers, but under conditions controlled by the producers. This mild British version of continental syndicalism was destroyed by the 1920s slump in which workers were exploited by wage cuts, longer hours and unemployment. But the ideas were important – the emphasis on industrial democracy and the needs of the consumers, which were lost when the Labour Party turned to state ownership and the benefits of the producers.

Both Beatrice and Sidney Webb turned away from the guild socialists and their continental counterparts. Beatrice Webb supervised the control of industry inquiry, which was clearly designed to provide the Fabian answer to the challenge of the syndicalists. She wrote in a memorandum,

> The object of our inquiry is to work out ... the main lines on which the control and management of industry and commerce by which the nation lives ... we can combine the widest measure of personal freedom and initiative with the maximum democratic control: the largest national product with an equalised distribution of commodities and services amongst the whole people. (Radice, p. 207).

They also argued that the material resources of the country had to run for the public rather than private profit and the nationalization of the mines, railways, iron and steel industries not just on ideological grounds but because as so many regulations already existed which caused friction between government and capital, nationalization would eliminate that. Public ownership was seen as a pragmatic and necessary tool of government.

These views were probably more acceptable to the unions than they might otherwise have been because of the impact of war. McKibben notes in his *History of the Labour Party* that everyone was more or less affected by wartime collectivism; even those unions suspicious of the state were impressed by its power (p. 58). It is worth noting that the Party both produced its socialist objective of common ownership, interpreted as state ownership, and implemented it in the aftermath of war, at a time when a collectivist approach was dominant.

But, despite the pragmatism contained in Sidney Webb's words and in the flexibility of the original statement to the first Labour Pary conference of June 1918, Webb still described 'common ownership' (meaning state ownership) as the distinguishing feature of socialism. It is misleading to describe this as the touchstone of socialism. The form of ownership should not be the distinguishing feature, but the ideals or aims underlying any change of ownership should be. The socialist aim is to achieve equality at work in terms of rewards, conditions and control both of capital and production. It is one means amongst others of achieving a more equal and just society. Different forms of common ownership may be more or less effective methods at different times for achieving equality. If Webb simply means that no other party is committed to state ownership of the means of production, then that may be true. It can, however, blind socialists into believing that achieving state ownership is the same as achieving socialism, when it is not. Changing ownership is a means to an end, not an end in itself. This confusion of means with ends can be seen when we look at what the Labour Party eventually did in government about state ownership.

The Labour Party had little opportunity to put Clause 4 into practice in its times in office in the 1920s. In January 1924 Labour came into power briefly when it combined with the Liberals to vote Stanley Baldwin, the Prime Minister, out of office. It was simply a caretaker administration, lasting only a few months, in which Labour had no overall majority. Labour lost the 1924 General Election but managed to form a minority government in 1929 under Ramsay Macdonald's leadership, which he turned into the National Government in 1931.

In the twenties, Labour had not emphasized its commitment. Only the nationalization of the coal mines appeared on the Party manifestos in the years up to 1929, and the second Macdonald government elected then made no effort to implement it. It was not through lack of detailed plans. The precise method of nationalization had been worked out by Frank Hodges, the then secretary of the Miners' Federation of Great Britain, and R. Tawney at the time of the Sankey Commission.

After the election defeat of 1931, the Party began to prepare more detailed plans, such as the TUC's *Public Control and Regulation of Industry and Trade* (1932). The ideas for these were first explored in a series of Fabian pamphlets and in the work of the National Fabian Research Bureau. Other models for public ownership emerged in the 1930s, such as the existence of the Central Electricity Board and the proposals for the public ownership of the electricity supply industry offered by the McGowan Committee appointed in 1936. All of this led to the list of items proposed for nationalization in 'Labour's Immediate Programme' of 1937. The list included the Bank of England, coal mines, electricity, gas, railways and 'other transport services', with some reference to the public ownership of land. The latter disappeared from the 1945 manifesto and was replaced with plans for the control of land use and development put forward in the 1942 Uthwatt Report, which was implemented by Lewis Silkin in the 1945 Government. Nationalization of the joint stock banks also disappeared.

Putting common ownership into practice

The opportunity to put public ownership into practice came with the massive Labour victory of 1945. The programme was essentially the same as that laid down in the original policy statement, *Labour and the New Social Order*. Subsequent Party conferences had elaborated it but its key proposals – nationalization of the public utilities and certain natural resources, public control of industry and egalitarian taxation plans – were restated in the 1945 document, *Let us Face the Future*. Additions to the 1937 manifesto were the nationalization of iron and steel, following the unanimous adoption of the Mikardo resolution in favour of public ownership at the 1944 Party conference. The Heyworth Committee called for the public ownership of the gas industry in its December 1945 report, and the Swinton plan for non-competing public airways. Public ownership was central in the 1945 manifesto in a way in which it has never been since, even in the lengthy 1983 manifesto. It was not surprising that this should be so, given six years of war in which the Party and its leadership had become accustomed to state ownership and control, and the population had learned to accept that state control was essential to secure a fair distribution of goods and services.

The 1945 Government then embarked on a major programme of nationalization. By the autumn of 1946, the state ownership of the Bank of England, civil aviation, cable and wireless, and coal mining were all on the statute book. There was very little opposition, either from the Conservative Parliamentary Party, who had in some cases argued for nationalization themselves in order to eliminate wasteful private competition (civil aviation), or from the public. Nationalization of the coal mines was helped by the generous, many would say over-generous, compensation paid to stock-holders. It was greeted by mass demonstrations of delighted miners on vesting day, 1 January 1947, in mining areas from South Wales to Nottingham, Yorkshire, Durham and Fife, when they saw the National Coal Board flag flying over the mines. In spite of the difficulties faced by the industry, the heritage from private ownership, a serious shortage of manpower, the 1947 fuel shortage, temporary stoppages and go-slows, it began to be profitable and productive. Output per manshift reached the highest ever levels. Industrial relations undoubtedly improved for gas, coal, electricity, civil aviation, steel, cable and wireless and railways after a poor start.

But better industrial relations were not enough. Disillusionment with nationalization soon set in. By the spring of 1948, Emmanuel Shinwell, then Chairman of Conference, was to say at the Scarborough Party conference defensively that 'we do not acquiesce in the view that nationalization in its present form is adequate for our purpose'.

The electricity supply industry was taken into public ownership in August 1947, helped by the overwhelming technical arguments of the McGowan Committee on the grounds of efficiency. It would lead to the integration of the national grid system, ensuring a nation-wide distribution of energy from a national system, with an interconnected transmission system operating on a standard voltage. Even before World War II, the majority of electricity services were under municipal control, so the transfer to full national control seemed quite natural.

Road and rail transport were also nationalized in 1947, but this time part of the Government's plans hit opposition both from the Tories and from the industry. Taking road haulage into public ownership included small road operators. The Conservatives took up their cause. The small operators with the 'C' licence used their vehicles to cover journeys of under forty miles. The Government's plans were presented as an invasion of individual liberty. The Government did give way, but only after a bitter struggle in the Lords Committee.

The final nationalization measure was the gas industry, completed after a long Parliamentary battle in May 1949. The intellectual ground had been prepared by the Heyworth Committee Report which had provided an impartial blueprint for the industry. Once again, it was comparatively easy to superimpose a national board on an industry already to a large extent in municipal ownership.

The main programme of nationalization was complete. All that remained was to take iron and steel into public ownership, but this led to real controversy in the industry and in Government. To start with, it was quite different from nationalizing the various public services. Nationalizing this manufacturing industry would inevitably involve engineering, machine tools and other metallurgical trades. Steel could not be described as 'failing the nation' either, as coal and railways had done. Steel-workers and their union were as cool towards nationalization then as they are now. But the industry urgently required new capital investment and rationalization and so the Government set up the Iron and Steel Board to this end, though it was also described as a prelude to public ownership. Some members of the Cabinet wanted it postponed; others were against it altogether, and one Labour MP even left the Party over the issue. Part of the reason for the Cabinet's hesitation was due to the fact that it was the first manufacturing industry to be nationalized. Eventually a compromise was reached. It meant having a Parliamentary Bill to reduce the Lords' delaying powers to a year so that the Iron and Steel Bill could be taken in the 1948–9 Parliamentary session. The bill became law at the end of 1949, with its commencement date postponed until 1 January 1951.

The Labour Party, with some notable exceptions, such as Ian Mikardo in his Fabian pamphlet *The Second Five Years: A Labour Programme for 1950*, had reached the limits of the nationalization programme. Even Aneurin Bevan, in a National Executive Committee discussion on the policy document *Socialism and Private Enterprise*, said, 'What we have to do is to create the framework within which private enterprise can operate efficiently.' By 1949, *Labour Believes in Britain*, its policy document for the election, emphasized the importance of the next election, but even so the 1950 election campaign manifesto included a 'shopping list' of industries to be nationalized, of which sugar refining was one of the items. 'Mr

Cube', calling for 'Tate [Tate and Lyle] not the state', appeared on everyone's sugar packets, an extremely useful propaganda weapon for the Tories. It gave them the chance for a well-organized and effective publicity campaign against nationalization, which helped to discredit it.

By then at least one-fifth of the nation's economy was in public ownership, but at last a coherent argument could be developed for the state holding of the basic utilities. The 'shopping list' approach inevitably implies justifying the nationalization of each particular item on the list in terms of the failings of the industry concerned. It is always easy to add to such a list, which can easily become a long one. It usually lacks any cohesion. No overall plan to develop the economy, especially the potential wealth-creating sectors lies behind the shopping lists.

By contrast, the 1945 election manifesto set out specific purposes to be achieved by nationalization in terms of their overall goals or the economy, that is, full employment and modernization. The Bank of England was to be taken over to ensure full employment. 'Public ownership of the fuel and power industries' would bring 'great economies in operation and make it possible to modernise production methods and raise safety standards in every colliery'. The public ownership of 'gas and electricity undertakings' would 'lower charges, prevent competitive waste, open the way for co-ordinated distribution'. The manifesto also stressed the overwhelming importance of public ownership for transport. 'The co-ordination of transport services for rail, road, air and canal cannot be achieved without unification. And unification without public transport means a steady struggle with sectional interests or the enthronement of a private monopoly, which would be a menace to the rest of industry.'

These arguments were presented in Parliament as well, though as time went on it was decided that it might not be politic to be too explicit. This caution resulted from the difficulties the Government faced over the iron and steel nationalization. John Wilmot, the then Minister of Supply, in a paper to the Cabinet supporting immediate nationalization, wrote, 'It is in my view fundamentally wrong to divorce control from ownership' (quoted by H. Pelling, *The Labour Government, 1945–51*, London, 1971, p. 83).

The new Minister of Supply, George Strauss, was actually responsible for introducing the bill to nationalize iron and steel, by taking over the stock of selected firms, rather than reorganizing the whole industry. In presenting the arguments for the bill to Cabinet, he referred to cartels and restrictive practices in the inter-war period and stated that 'rationalisation, the elimination of wasteful competition, and proper industrial planning would be possible' (quoted in ibid., p. 85).

The Cabinet, however, wished to underplay some of the arguments. Domination by financial interests, for example, was not to be overstressed, because those same interests had been responsible for such modernization of the industry as had taken place during the inter-war years. So the arguments which Strauss actually presented during the debate on the bill were that it would enable steel to 'become an efficient national instrument for planning full employment ... offer greater security to those who work in it. It will enable our home consumers to get the steel they require at low cost' (p. 458, HC Deb 53–78 15 Nov. 1948). Subsequent events have shown that the public ownership of steel alone could not possibly fulfil those aims. Herbert Morrison, in winding up the debate, took up the issue of breaking up the cartels and made that his argument. But it is not necessary to take industries into public ownership to get that result; effective anti-trust legislation would be much more useful, something which the Labour Government neglected (for a fuller account of the arguments over the nationalization of steel within the Labour Party, see Pelling, pp. 88 ff.).

Public ownership soon run into criticisms from the Labour movement itself. Much of the criticism rightly condemned the lack of industrial democracy, as well as the appointment to the Boards of industrialists and others with no knowledge of the particular industry concerned and no commitment to public service, a feature which has plagued the nationalized industries since their inception.

But neither Herbert Morrison nor the TUC intended state ownership to be a means of extending industrial democracy. Morrison argued strongly against such an approach and his views were shared by the TUC in its *Interim Report on Reconstruction* in 1944.

> It will be essential, not only for the maintenance and improvement of the standards and conditions of the work-people, but because of the power of independent criticisms they can exert, that they shall maintain their complete independence. They can hardly do so if they are compromised in regard to Board decisions which are not considered to be in their members' interests by the fact of their representatives' participation in them.

The denial of any extension of industrial democracy soon met with opposition from the Party. These views were not shared by individual trade union leaders or by the rank and file members of the trade unions or the Party.

At the 1948 Party conference, J. B. Figgins, Secretary of the National Union of Railways, after welcoming the nationalization of the railways, said that the men 'should have the opportunity of appointment to managerial or supervisory positions. Only in that way are we going to get any co-operation between the managerial and supervisory side and those who are supervised' (*Labour Party Conference Report*, pp. 168–9). A year later his views were supported by a rank and file guardsman. He complained that the old managers had retained control and that the industry was burdened with heavy compensation payments. He wanted to 'place the workers in control of the railways'. The National Union of Railways had also published the results of their survey of railwaymen's views after nationalization in the *Railway Review*, December 1949. This showed that 45 per cent of the respondents thought their jobs had been virtually unchanged by public ownership, 45 per cent thought that frustration had increased and fewer than 15 per cent felt that they had a share in the running of the railways. Similar views were expressed in other resolutions to Party conference; sixteen in the 1948 conference and fourteen in the 1949 conference called for the democratic control of nationalized industries and more socialists on the Boards.

Though industrial relations had improved vastly, nevertheless the conduct of labour relations left much to be desired. Troops were used to unload ships; emergency resolutions were applied, and the Government even agreed to renew the Emergency Powers Act, brought in by the Lloyd George Government in 1920. The fundamental relations between unions and management had not changed. This led Margaret Cole to call for a new system of 'human relations' in the nationalized industries.

Others were even more critical. The *New Statesman* kept a watch on the progress of public ownership. It commented that, in spite of the enthusiasm with which nationalization of the coal mines was received in 1948, miners felt that nothing had changed under the new regime, and that, in general, the public Boards seemed to many workers to resemble large firms such as Levers or ICI. 'The boards are remote from the ordinary worker, and the representatives of management with whom he comes into direct contact are nearly all the same persons as before' (*New Statesman*, 28 August 1948, p. 37). By 1950, the *New Statesman* echoed the now popular demand within the Party to 'socialise the nationalised industries'. That theme has been reiterated down the years since then. But successive Labour Governments have manifestly failed to democratize the nationalized industries, though there have been limited attempts at encouraging participation. Small wonder then that there has been so little opposition to privatization.

Furthermore, although John Wilmot as Minister of Supply had talked about the necessity of ownership for the sake of control of industry, the Government did not use the publicly owned industries as a lever for further direction or control of the economy, or make the industries answerable to the Government, Parliament, or, of course, the workers.

The Government believed that it faced a 'financial Dunkirk' and that the managerial and technical skills to deal with the crisis could only be found in private industry. There was little attempt to plan the economy. Any reference to that approach was conspicuously absent from the 1945 manifesto, despite references to a 'national plan' and the commitment to full employment, to be achieved through partial nationalization; the full utilization of national resources; the provision of good wages; social services; tax policy and planned investment. The only direction the the Labour Party really had in mind was the continuation of war-time physical and financial controls, to help exports, to direct industry towards development areas and to direct the use of vital raw materials. Planning was also regarded with some suspicion.

The 1947 Economic Survey distinguished between 'totalitarian and democratic planning', and although in war-time the people had given their government the 'power to direct labour', that would not happen in normal times. 'A democratic government must therefore conduct its economic planning in a manner which preserves the maximum freedom of choice to the individual citizen.' Methods of compulsion over labour or capital were regarded as impractical and contrary to the freedom of the individual.

The 'system' of planning proposed in the Economic Survey consisted of three elements:

1. An organisation with enough knowledge and reliable information to assess our national resources and to formulate national needs.

2. A set of economic 'budgets' which relate these needs to our resources, and which enable the government to say what is the best use of resources in the national interest.

3. A number of methods, the combined effect of which will enable the government to influence the use of resources in the desired direction, without interfering with democratic freedom.

But at the same time the Government had no facilities for long-term planning, few economists and statisticians, no forecasts or up-to-date surveys of industry, production or manpower, and no Minister or Department to implement or devise these long-term plans.

The Lord President's Committee, set up in 1947, chaired by Herbert Morrison and including Hugh Dalton and Sir Stafford Cripps among others, became the main method of planning, and was soon shown to be woefully inadequate. It failed to deal with the coal shortages or the balance of payments crisis of 1947. In fact, far from being able to deal with such crises, the Committee was apt to reject any arguments for planning in some key areas. War-time controls were retained at least for the first few years after the war, but these were quite inappropriate for the post-war reconstruction and development of the economy. The Government failed to develop any suitable means of planning. Meanwhile Britain's main competitors planned their post-war reconstruction, and an opportunity was lost.

No overall direction was given to the industries under public ownership nor were they answerable to Parliament. Prime Minister Clement Attlee had invited Morrison to provide a Parliamentary written answer in 1947, which laid down the questions MPs could ask about nationalized industries. Morrison replied that since the Government was not responsible for the 'day-to-day' administration, a Minister could only answer questions about 'any directions he [gives] in the national interest, and for any action he [takes] on proposals which a Board [is] required by statute to lay before him'. Debate would not be allowed on the 'annual reports and accounts which are to be laid before Parliament.' (HCDeb. 568 4 Dec. 1947). MPs did not find that answer particularly satisfying then, nor have they since, but apart from select committee investigations nothing else has changed, except, of course, the number of industries for which the Minister has some sort of responsibility.

The fact is that the programme of nationalization, massive though it was, was carried through Parliament apparently with little thought being given to the purpose of ownership and with no coherent framework into which the nationalized industries fitted and in which they would have a specific role to play as state-owned industries. State ownership by itself does not constitute a planned economy nor redistribute income and wealth, which was after all the main point of the exercise in terms of the Party's constitution. That much is clear from the experience of the 1945–51 Labour Governments.

Even in the public sector, coal, gas and the other industries operated quite separately from each other, directed solely by their own Boards. There was no attempt to provide an integrated transport system, for example, a limited piece of economic planning, something which the Party has talked about for a long time but has never seriously put into practice.

The potential of controlling 20 per cent of the economy for planning the economy as a whole was never exploited by the post-war Government or subsequently. The 1960s Labour Governments told the nationalized industries 'to operate at minimum cost, earn reasonable profits, and in general behave commercially, at least in the sense of behaving as if they were operating under conditions of imperfect competition, which is what a marginal cost approach to pricing and investment really means' (R. Pryke, *The Nationalised Industries: Policies and Performance since 1968*, Oxford, 1981, p. 262).

In the 1970s they were expected to pursue a 'variety of goals (under both governments) which have often been contradictory and seldom of long duration' (ibid.). These demoralized the industries, lowered management morale and reduced their sense of responsibility. Sir Richard Marsh, who presided over the British Rail financial debacle, for example, according to Pryke 'blames the government and never even considers that his policies were mistaken' (ibid., p. 263).

The public debate over recent years has focused on whether the state-owned industries are efficient or not. Pryke has a somewhat gloomy view but even he allows that

> it would be wrong to attribute the nationalised industries' failings simply to public ownership. Almost any collection of British industries would have shown up badly ... bad management and poor labour relations are by no means confined to the public enterprise sector ... the operation of industries that belong to the public sector poses particular problems because they tend to be natural monopolies and/or be in decline. Any of the weaknesses which appear to the British experience to be a consequence of public ownership are displayed by the same industries abroad under private ownership. (ibid., p. 265)

He cites the German and Belgian coal industries, privately owned but heavily subsidized, as examples.

Others take a less pessimistic view; for example, in 1986, in presenting a memorandum to the Energy Select Committee, the trade unions representing employees in British Gas were able to demonstrate that it had more than matched the financial requirements laid down by the Department of Energy, achieving rates of growth well above the Government's targets. These results could no doubt be reduplicated by other state-owned concerns.

But the argument about the efficiency or otherwise of the publicly owned industries, important though it is, is not to the point here. The very fact that the whole debate turned on efficiency or lack of it, and that for the public every failure – a late train or the gas man not turning up for an appointment – was enough to condemn the whole public sector, shows the extent to which public ownership had become an end in itself, not a means. The Party had lost sight of the whole purpose of common ownership as set out in Clause 4. Efficiency is important, of course, but nationalization was not just about creating efficient enterprises.

Many socialists realized that the Morrisonian style state-owned industries did not fulfil the goal of the 'best obtainable system of popular administration and control', so there were experiments with workers' representation on Boards, in the Post Office and the steel industry. British Gas developed a system of negotiation and consultation through a management/trade union planning liaison committee, where long-term trends as well as strategic planning of the industry are discussed and information is given to employees, as far as possible, about future plans. There was a great deal of discussion about industrial democracy in the 1970s, but little progress was made in the state-owned industries or in industry generally.

State ownership was designed to achieve important socialist objectives of equality and freedom for the individual. It did not. Denationalization was never, in spite of the Government's protestations, intended to achieve any such aims. It is impossible to see how re-nationalization can take place, given the sheer scale and costs of the enterprise. Re-purchase is not a popular option, by whatever means. Labour's priorities on taking office will inevitably be with industry and employment, health, education and housing.

Privatization has one and only one merit. It has cleared the decks. It forces us to clarify the distinction between principles and policies. The principles of Clause 4 remain unchanged. Other modes of sharing profits and accumulated capital with employees are available. These should be examined and adapted to conditions in Britain.

The key to our approach should by 'empowerment'. It is astonishing how the founding fathers of the Labour Party and the post-war Labour Governments, aided and abetted by the official representatives of the trade union movement, had so little respect for the working classess and so little faith in their ability. Elitism of that kind has no place in socialism today; so policies must allow greater control over the environment, housing and the work-place and must address that difficult task of finding workable and effective frameworks.

Economic planning was not part of the objectives of state ownership as described in the Labour Party's constitution. The

Attlee Government first carried out its programme of nationalization and only then turned it attention to planning the economy. During the fifties, the ideas of state ownership and industrial strategy became inextricably linked, as Aneurin Bevan began to define the limits of nationalization as the 'commanding heights' of the economy. These heights were at first dominated by coal and steel, aircraft and shipbuilding. As these ceased to be the engines of growth, the Party's attention turned to other possibilities for public ownership, and so the 'shopping list' approach developed. It reflects the fact that state ownership is not an essential condition for planning.

The world has moved on since 1945. The growing dominance of industry by multinationals makes owning part of such an enterprise irrelevant. Increasing dependence on international trade and the globalization of the world's financial markets make successful economic management much more difficult; nationalizing an industry does not insulate it from foreign competition. So achieving the kind of economic management we want, expressing the ideals contained in Clause 4, requires new and imaginative instruments of management. Here we should learn from the experience of successful socialist countries, such as Sweden, and even from non-socialist but planned economies, such as Japan. In the following chapters, we shall examine various models of common ownership to learn from the successes and failures of other socialist countries.

Chapter 3
Co-operatives

There have always been three strands in British socialist thought about alternatives to or restraints upon capitalist ownership: co-operative production; strengthening trade union and consumer co-operatives; and state socialism, the latter emerging in the 1870s. The term 'common ownership' was accepted as covering both the older co-operative ideas of Robert Owen, François Fourier and Ferdinand Lassalle and the newer ideas of state socialists. It was used in the Gotha programme of the German Social Democratic Party in 1875, in the constitution of the Independent Labour Party in 1892 and in the Labour Party's constitution of 1918. It is entirely possible that the term was selected to allow for the development of all or any of these strands, though the Webbs themselves saw state socialism as the way ahead.

Co-operative ownership constitutes a long-standing and respected form of common ownership. It can be seen as a form of 'private ownership' in that co-operatives are independent of the state, and therefore avoid the problems of the concentration of state power, but it is a form of common ownership that can cover state, municipal and co-operative ownership. Since individual members of a co-operative share in the profits and management of the enterprise, they are seen as a 'third way' between the concentration of state power through public ownership and the exploitation of labour by capitalism.

In recent years, there has been a revival of interest in industrial co-operatives, both in Britain and in many other countries, just because they are seen as the 'third way', as something different from state ownership or private capitalist ownership. It is also due to the recognition that industrial co-operatives can contribute to the reduction of unemployment. It is a way in which the unemployed can, with the support of some public funds, provide themselves with jobs.

Here again, Britain can learn from other countries. The Italian producer co-operative sector is the largest in Western Europe with about 80 per cent of the total number of co-operatives in the European Community. In 1981, it was composed of about 1,200 co-operatives employing about half a million people. They are mainly located in Emilia-Romagna, Lombardy and Tuscany, and operate in construction and services. Italian co-operatives have benefited from strong central organizations such as Lega, a federation of co-operatives linked to the Socialist and Communist parties, public work contracts from local authorities and from combines of co-operatives formed to deal with finance, design and marketing. They are often large, with an average of over three hundred workers in the top 10 per cent of firms, a sharp contrast with Britain in which the new co-operatives are often very small.

In 1982, the French co-operative sector had about 40,000 workers in about 1,200 co-operatives, with well-established firms in printing, construction and engineering. The co-operative sector there has the advantage of a clear legal framework and tax incentives.

But, in Britain, the industrial co-operative sector is very small. It now comprises about 1,500 businesses with an estimated combined turnover of £200 million a year. The sector suffers from a shortage of capital even though there is good evidence to show that co-operatives have a better survival rate than conventional small businesses. This is shown by an examination of the loans to co-operatives by the Industrial Common Ownership Finance (ICOF), the best known source of funding for co-operatives, which has an annual write-off rate of only 10 per cent for the loans it makes, comparing very favourably with commercial bank experience on bad debts with small firms in general. That result is born out in survey work conducted by Dr S. Estrin and V. Perotin, published as 'Co-operatives and participatory firms in Great Britain' in the *International Review of Applied Economics*, Vol. 62, No. 12, March 1987.

The ICOF has been lending to co-operatives for fifteen years, and has lent more than £1 million to over a hundred co-ops from its own revolving loan fund and the funds it administers for such regional authorities as the West Midlands and West Glamorgan County Councils. Typically the ICOF lends amounts between £7,500 and £10,000 over periods ranging from six months to six years. The average loan is £7,000 and the minimum £1,000 on the security of the co-operatives business assets in the form of a fixed and floating charge. Repayments are made regularly throughout the life of the loan with interest on the balance, with the rate of interest held steady over the life of the loan and at levels below that demanded by the main clearing banks. This is one source of funds for the co-operatives in Britain; others being local authorities, local co-operative development agencies, the London Co-operative Development Fund and Co-operative Venture Capital (Scotland). Another source of funds for small co-operatives is the enterprise allowance scheme, which provides £40 a week for each individual who meets the eligibility conditions, but which will not be paid if the proposed co-operative has more than ten members.

A future Labour Government could ensure that these sources of finance for co-operatives, to which the main banks are somewhat reluctant to extend loans, because on conventional banking criteria they tend to be highly geared, have adequate finance available. The rules could be made more flexible, and perhaps more generous allowances could be made available under the enterprise allowance scheme. Many more training schemes for co-operative workers in business management and accountancy must be made available if there is to be a substantial and thriving co-operative sector. The investment would be worthwhile in view of their superior survival rate.

However some forms of co-operatives would be more difficult to help. The Industrial Common Ownership Movement, for example, has very strict rules; outside shareholders are not allowed. Indeed, there are no shares at all beyond the nominal £1 entry fee. These co-operatives do not attract conventional loans and many are in 'alternative' activities such as producing wholefoods. Pay is notoriously low, and many survive only by interest-free loans from members and friends. Without financial incentives to accumulate, they will not grow and would continue to require public support. This is not the only problem faced by co-operatives. They often suffer from the image of failure acquired by the collapse of the three co-operatives set up to take over ailing companies in the 1970s. The three buy-outs encouraged by the Labour Government of 1974–9, Kirkby Manufacturing, Meriden Triumph and the Scottish Daily Press, have not survived. They were all very weak firms, and were initially underfunded. Kirkby's failure was also due to poor labour relations and the inability to decide on rationalization and redundancy. An industrial co-operative usually has two forms of communication: a committee of management or board of directors selected by workers, and the usual information, consultation and representation through trade union machinery. In Kirkby Manufacturing and Engineering there was no such distinction between representative and executive roles. Co-operative democracy cannot work through trade union machinery. Meriden ran into design and marketing problems as well. The *Scottish Daily News* venture received a Government loan of up to one half of the capital costs, up to a maximum of £1.75 million, but the workers had to find the rest of the money from non-Governmental sources, and to show prospective lenders the Government's Industrial Development Unit report, which had concluded that the success of the venture was very remote. It was obviously difficult to raise money in these circumstances, so the workers put in their own savings and bought the plant and buildings with the aid of Robert Maxwell's commercial expertise. Unfortunately, the newspaper lasted for only six months, and the workers lost both their jobs and savings.

It is unfortunate that more care was not taken over the establishment of workers' co-operatives in the 1970s. Although the number of co-operatives has grown from less than twenty in 1975 to 1,600 in 1987, employing over ten thousand people, the average size was about five workers. They are concentrated in the service sector, bookshops, printing, restaurants, etc., with a turn-over of less than £100,000 in the main. Any plans to promote them by a future Labour Government, by increasing the funds available to the ICOF and other bodies, must ensure that proper criteria for lending to viable projects continue to be followed. It is not to anyone's advantage, and especially that of the the workers involved, to raise hopes for employment and profits, only to find that the project collapses six months later.

Labour would have to stress the success of the co-operatives now operating in the United Kingdom, and those abroad. But it is worth considering one of the most famous examples briefly.

Mondragon

Perhaps it is not surprising that attention has focused on the Mondragon experiment ever since it was first drawn to the attention of a wider audience in 1978 by R. Oakeshott in his book *The Case for Worker Co-operatives*. It is unique in Europe in terms of size, growth, range of production activities and to the extent it is integrated with local communities; it is more extensive than co-operatives typically found in capitalist countries. It was founded by Father Arzmendi, a priest, who had at one stage fled from Franco's forces, when he had worked on *Eguna*, an anti-Franco trade union paper. He was sent to Mondragon when the German occupation prevented him from continuing his studies in Belgium. He was influenced by Robert Owen's ideas and the principles adopted by the Rochdale Pioneers, a trade unionist Christian socialist group, who founded the first successful co-operative in Britain in 1844. He set up the first factory in Mondragon with five of his own students, engineeering apprentices. The factory, Ulgor, produced paraffin heaters and cookers.

The problems they faced, including limited access to finance, led them to set up a co-operative savings bank, the Caja Laboral Popular, in 1959. By 1980, it had 300,000 deposit accounts covering individuals and manufacturing co-operatives, providing capital to be invested in the co-operative group. There are more than eighty industrial co-operatives, employing some 17,000 people in manufacturing machine tools, refrigerators, furniture, bicycles, electrical components, computers and bus bodies. Social security needs are provided by another co-operative, Lagun Aro, and training by Alecoop, a co-operative factory and training school, which particularly encourages training amongst girls.

Mondragon has made every effort to keep up with foreign competition by setting up a common research and development co-operative, Ikerlan, in 1977 at a cost of $12 million. Amongst other activities, Ikerlan has designed its own industrial robot, Gizamat.

The Mondragon Group has been consistently profitable (see H. Thomas and C. Logan, *Mondragon: An Economic Analysis*, London, 1982). The individual co-operatives have a sizeable market share in certain products, up to 30 per cent for some consumer durables. They are not large enterprises because of the decision to avoid increasing the staff beyond 500, the optimum level for co-operative managment. By 1979 the share of exports in total sales had risen to 18 per cent and increased again to 33 per cent in 1985, with total sales being valued at 140.9 million pesetas and exports at 32.9 million pesetas in that year. Mondragon was affected both by Spain's membership of the European Community, and by the recession of the early 1980s. But, by comparison with other Basque industries, Mondragon's adjustment was apparently more flexible and less costly in terms of jobs. Pay was held back and a cautious borrowing policy resulted in cuts in real capital formation, which was halved between 1977 and 1983. But jobs were saved, 17,000 in 1985, up by 233 from 1984, and Mondragon continues to flourish.

The co-operative has a Board of Directors, elected by all members of the co-operative on a one person one vote basis. The Board selects the management, but the workers are able to influence the management through the Social Council. The latter is elected by a group of ten workers, each of which elects a representative to the Social Council which serves in an advisory capacity to management and the Board. The Management Council is an advisory and consultative group nominated by management and the Board, and meets at least once a month.

Strictly speaking the co-operative does not pay wages, but advances out of anticipated profits. To attract employees, these were somewhat higher than those of surrounding firms but the range of wages between the highest and the lowest workers in the co-operatives is of the ratio of 1 to 5. An individual's pay is determined according to specific criteria, taking into account qualifications, responsibilities, especially hard or dangerous work and 'social integration'. There have been pay disputes, which of course create special tensions in a co-operative. Workers also receive a share of profits, both individually and through the Social Fund, according to set formulae. Although there is no guarantee of life-long employment, every effort is made to absorb those made redundant by redeployment.

In addition, surpluses are distributed to individual accounts in the form of capital, not bonuses. Individual accounts bear most of the fluctuation in profitability under the Mondragon rules so that the link between profits and incentives is assured. Individual accumulated profits cannot be withdrawn until retirement, making them closer to stock options to be exercised in the future.

Like most co-operatives, Mondragon screens would-be co-operators, and those selected are thoroughly trained in the co-operative approach and in understanding the nature of the enterprise they have joined. Features of Mondragon which contribute to its success are the emphasis on the up-grading of technical skills and socialization into a specific ideology, with worker ownership as an alternative means to generate consensus and integrate the work-force. It adjusts to market changes through internal labour flexibility and this in turn generates the necessary loyalty from worker owners. It is hardly surprising that such loyalty is much more difficult to obtain in companies where workers are regarded as expendable.

The collective bargaining arrangements in Mondragon are plainly altered by the fact that all members play a part in setting pay relativities in each plant and in formulating and applying disciplinary rules. Differentials are narrow, but promotion can be rapid. This is because Mondragon has difficulty in recruiting experienced managers. Their jobs are enriched to provide an incentive for them to remain in the group.

Management faces problems at best not explicit in conventional firms.

> When a manager is not performing well the co-operators soon get rid of him. Co-operators believe that mangement must resolve problems and if they don't, they're changed. ... Managers must succeed in order to maintain their jobs. Managers have often to justify their policies before the Junta Rectora and the collective. (Keith Bradley and Alan Gelb, *Co-operation at Work: The Mondragon Experience*, 1983, p. 62)

Worker shareholders are likely to exert a more effective influence on their management than conventional corporate shareholder, because they are less dispersed and do not vote by proxy as directed by the Board. Because they are inside the firm, they have better access to information than most shareholders and are perhaps more aware of management errors. A critical attitude to management is something shared with workers in conventional firms, but of course they have little opportunity to influence decisions, no matter how conscious they are of the obvious failings of top-heavy management – 'more chiefs than Indians'. It is true that management in co-operatives may be criticized unfairly, but at least its decisions and policies can be influenced by the members. Accountability to workers is strongly resisted by management in conventional firms as eroding their 'right to manage'. Innovations such as quality circles show that labour is anxious to contribute its detailed knowledge of production processes to raise efficiency – a threat to middle management in particular who are not supposed to be accountable to subordinates. In Mondragon this accountability is rigorous. But conventional firms especially lose a great deal of knowledge and expertise, which could be tapped to everyone's advantage, and fail to involve workers in the enterprise because of the refusal to consult with the work-force.

Mondragon's contribution

Examination of the Mondragon experiment shows that industrial relations are generally good, and that there is a close link between consensus and productivity. Co-operative organization can often be extremely efficient. Some would argue that the model is best suited to re-industrialization and that 'it might serve as a catalyst for regional development or regeneration' (ibid., p.83). Strong local attachments are also important in preserving managerial talent. This means that co-operatives may play an important role in redeveloping the regions which have suffered from the de-industrialization of recent years, provided they are not used in a futile attempt to revive declining industries, in which British labour costs, however modest, cannot and should not be low enough to enable Britain to compete with newly developed countries and their new capital investment. Since the co-operatives should be in new industries, they will require full training and retraining facilities to be provided, not just in new skills, but also in co-operative principles. Mondragon rightly spends much time and effort on this area.

This is one of the most important reasons for encouraging the development of industrial co-operatives. Common ownership helps to increase managerial efficiency, because management is account-able to worker members. This accountability enables workers to identify with the enterprise for which they work as does their participation in the bonuses resulting from increased efficiency. Workers may be consulted and provided with information and be represented in conventional companies. The representative bodies may sometimes have effective power, but it takes co-operative ownership to make management formally responsible to the workers and not to outside shareholders.

Successful though the Mondragon experience is, it may be difficult to translate it into the British economy, with its shrinking industrial sector dominated by large companies and institutional shareholdings. On the other hand, the same companies have often been reluctant to move into high technology, high risk ventures for which co-operatives may be well suited.

What can be learned from the Mondragon success is the thoroughness of professional market research, feasibility studies and training undertaken by their co-operative bank before a new co-operative is launched. They respond to the market and do not produce goods merely in response to social need. In Britain this would require closer links between banks with a co-operative history, producer co-operatives and more substantial Government funding. Currently co-operatives in the United Kingdom are most effective in low-tech service activities, which are labour intensive and require minimum capital. The co-operative sector would need to re-examine its rules and its attitude to outside finance in order to attract funds to finance more capital intensive co-operatives or to provide growth to the service sector. Training and education must not be ignored either as they are plainly an essential feature in Mondragon's prowess.

Other difficulties arise from the relationship between trade unions and co-operatives. Some unions, such as the TGWU and the AEU, have a commitment to promote co-operative production in their rules, but have been compelled to fight to maintain their members' living standards. The difficulties go deeper than that, since unions belong to the capitalist market economy, and collective bargaining for higher wages does not fit easily into a self-managed socio-economic system. They would have to fulfil a different function in relation to co-operatives and perhaps a representative organization of co-operatives on a national scale would have a useful role in preserving self-management.

Mobility of labour is problematic for co-operatives, especially the Mondragon variety. New entrants have to buy in so that members who wish to leave are able to sell their holdings on resignation. A high turn-over will concentrate share ownership among the long-established members of the group. There are other options; the Baxi Partnership model allows for only 40 per cent of the shares to be held individually, and the John Lewis Partnership allows only for bonuses rather than capital appreciation as a reward, the shares all being owned in a trust. Another way of dealing with the problem is to allow co-operatives to issue non-voting preference shares, as co-operatives in the United States and Canada do. The Industrial and Provident Societies Act would have to be amended acordingly.

It may not be easy to transfer the Mondragon model to British industry, but the problems are not insuperable. But those who wish to apply it must study all the conditions for Mondragon's expansion carefully. The provision of finance through its bank, the care taken before embarking on a new venture and the rigorous education and training of its members are vital ingredients.

Given the right conditions, Mondragon shows that it is possible to overcome the limitations on co-operatives in Britain. It has coped with the difficult feat of considering the welfare of its members, and surviving a period of recession with increased employment, and responded to changed market conditions brought about by Spain's entry to the European Community. Its product range has changed dramatically over the past thirty years, moving from low-tech paraffin heaters and cookers to computers and sophisticated machine tools. This has been achieved by providing its own source of finance. Any similar development in Britain will require co-operative banks, able to offer the necessary support and information services for the co-operative sector. Then and only then will the co-operatives be able to capture a substantial section of the productive sector.

Chapter 4
Employee Share Ownership

Employee share ownership schemes (often called ESOPS) can be seen as part of a long tradition in socialist thought – the idea that workers should own and control the enterprises in which they work. But employee share ownership schemes reflect a jumbled variety of aims and forms. It is important to disentangle these.

Some claim that wider employee share ownership will give people greater control over their lives and help them to achieve individual self-fulfilment, an aim with which the Marx of the Paris Manuscripts would have concurred. Others see it as another way of achieving a property-owning democracy, about which President Ronald Reagan once said, 'Could there be a better answer to the stupidity of Karl Marx than millions of workers individually sharing in the means of production' (quoted by R. Russell, *Using Ownership to Control: Making Workers Owners in the Contemporary United States*, p. 253, 1984). If they did, it might be. ESOPS are thus seen as a sop to the workers, provided they do not seriously challenge the concentration of ownership, as a way of preventing the onset of Marxism.

Other writers are interested only in the concrete results of employee share ownership in improving the performance of firms and industrial relations. Martin Weitzman argues in his *Share Economy: Conquering Stagflation* (Harvard University Press, 1984) that fixed wages should be replaced by value-added shares so that an individual employee's pay would be the labour share divided by the number of employees. The marginal cost of labour would be zero, so companies would compete to hire workers. It would be an alternative to Keynesian reflationary policies, or at least that is what Weitzman claims. Thus tax concessions of the order of 50 per cent exemption from corporation tax to stimulate profit-sharing would be justified in terms of falling unemployment. The shares in this case represent entitlements to shares of income rather than individual claims on equity; that is, they would receive lower wages but greater profit-sharing bonuses. Employees would be hired on the basis of maximizing returns on capital, but existing employees would have no say in that, since it would obviously clash with their aim of restricting the spread of bonuses so that bonus payments were as large as possible. Plainly there is nothing socialist about this approach to employee share ownership. It severely restricts workers' rights, gives them no control over the company and accentuates short-term interests because they cannot realize the capital value of their shares. It is an impractical proposition many companies would have to adopt profit-sharing at the same time, or competition to hire workers would not take place.

This is just one of the many forms employee share ownership may take, ranging from profit-sharing without any ownership of equity to management buy-outs, with the ownership restricted to a few managers or shares held in trust and incapable of being sold as with the John Lewis Partnership, or ESOPS in which the shares may be individually held and freely traded or traded only in special circumstances. The extent of ownership varies widely, too, from a 100 per cent share ownership by employees to shares held in individual accounts, or profit-related bonuses.

The control given to members of the firm can be anything from determining the broad strategic decisions to the organization of individual tasks; direct control through mass meetings or indirect through the election of a Board of Directors to whom management is accountable. Employees' power may be limited to vetoing decisions or extended to initiating policy.

Employee share or stock ownership schemes are a long-standing feature of the industrial scene in other countries, including Sweden, Japan and the United States, for example, providing a wealth of experience on which to draw. In the United States, the latest survey indicates that there are 8,100 ESOPS, covering over 8 million workers, about 7.3 per cent of non-agricultural workers, an increase from 1,600 covering 250,000 workers in 1974. In transportation, communications and utilities, 30 per cent of employees participated in ESOPS, and about 12 per cent in manufacturing. At current trends, a quarter of all American workers will own part or all of their companies by the year 2000.

ESOPS have flourished in the United States, partly because of special and generous tax concessions and sixteen laws, mainly the result of the work of Senator Russell B. Long, a Democrat, who chaired the Senate Finance Committee until 1981, to encourage their development. He was influenced by the works of Louis Kelso (for example, Louis O. Kelso and Mortimer J. Adler, The Capitalist Manifesto, New York, 1958). The tax breaks probably amounted to $2.5 billion in 1986. The tax credits include 1 per cent of new capital investment, introduced in 1975, extended by a further 0.5 per cent 'matching credit' with voluntary employee contributions; and then by 0.5 per cent of the payroll in 1983–7. The concentration of economic power has been a source of anxiety for all political parties in the United States in a way in which it has not been in Britain.

> In terms of stock ownership, about 1 per cent of our people own 50 per cent of it. About 6 per cent own 80 per cent, but the shocking part is that about 80 per cent of our people don't own any investment at all in productive wealth. That is something that concerns those of us who believe in a strong capitalist system. (Congressional Record, Vol. 127, No. 50, 27 March 1981)

ESOPS against this background are seen as extending the social basis of the ownership of assets, and of redistributing income at source through the distribution of asset ownership.

A number of surveys of the performance of ESOPS have been carried out. The most recent survey was carried out by Corey Rosen and Michael Quarry (in 'How well is employee ownership working?', *Harvard Business Review*, September-October 1987). One of its most important conclusions is that ESOPS companies 'that instituted participation plans grew at a rate three or four times faster than ESOPS companies that did not' (p. 128). In 1986, they studied forty-five ESOPS companies, taking into account the data for each of the five years before the ESOPS, and for five years afterwards, comparing them with similar conventional companies, all in the context of national trends for the industry concerned. The ESOPS companies' annual employment growth outstripped that of comparable companies by 5.05 per cent and their sales growth was 5.4 per cent faster. They conducted a randomly selected ESOPS in 1985, to determine how much the workers had profited in the previous four years. The average contribution was the equivalent of 10.1 per cent of workers' pay and the average annual gain was 11.5 per cent, compared with about 6 per cent for the Dow Jones industrial average during that period.

The history of employee ownership in the United States, as distinct from co-operatives, which date back to the eighteenth century there, began in the 1920s. The Illinois Central Railroad began to sell its stock to employees through a profit-sharing programme in 1899, followed by Proctor & Gamble in 1903. By 1929 it is estimated that about one million employees together owned in excess of $1 billion of stock, but the value of their shares was wiped out in the stock market crash, and the whole idea of employee share ownership, both on the part of the United States Government and, indeed, employees themselves, suffered a severe setback. Employees were also much more vulnerable under the schemes current in the 1920s. Some companies with employee stock plans sold shares without voting stock to employees, but many sold ordinary voting shares. The employee could sell the shares as an individual. These are quite unlike the present employee ownership plans, in which employees own stock in their company exclusively through a trust.

After the 1920s employee ownership schemes came to an end in the 1929 stock market crash, interest did not revive until in the 1970s with the passing of the Employee Retirement and Income Security Act 1975, which included a provision for ESOPS. The schemes that came into existence in the 1970s are different in two important ways from the earlier ones: employees do not receive the shares until they leave the company, nor do they purchase the shares; instead these are contributed to the trust by the company.

ESOPS are therefore seen by many of their supporters in the United States as a way of redistributing income by redistributing assets. They work by a company setting up an employee stock ownership trust (ESOT), which borrows loan capital to buy company stock. The company fully guarantees the trust. Each year the company may place up to 25 per cent of its wages bill into the ESOT to pay off the loan. Company shares are allocated to each employee's ESOP account as the loan is paid off. When employees leave or retire, they sell their shares back to the ESOP. New employees joining the firm also join the plan and start to build up their own share account.

One of the problems with American ESOPS is the way in which the tax concessions work, making the system open to abuse. ESOPS payments can replace other employee benefits, which do not attract the same generous tax reliefs. This encourages firms to replace an existing pension plan with an ESOPS so that investments made outside the company become part of its investment, and the firm buys its own shares at nil cost. Companies can also sell shares to their own employees at grossly inflated prices. This is a particular problem where companies have few outside owners of shares. In these cases, the company chooses consultants to select a formula for assessing the value of the shares from a wide range of possibilities. This gives the appearance of fairness, but, of course, the consultant's formula always leads to the most favourable price as far as the company is concerned. Plainly workers should have the right to take part in selecting the consultant and in assessing the formula to be used, or to provide their own consultants in such circumstances. Legislation introduced in the United Kingdom would have to be carefully drawn to avoid such misuses of the scheme.

Sometimes ESOPS have been used in open companies to build up a controlling voice for the management, to the exclusion of the work-force. The American experience suggests that many companies set up an ESOPS, but make few changes in their management practices, even to the extent of refusing to disclose information about sales, earnings and stock valuations to employee shareholders.

The use of pension funds to set up ESOPS, to prevent buy-outs and as a takeover defence strategy can lead to further alarming abuses. Dan River Textiles, one of America's largest textile firms, with over twelve thousand employees, is a case in point. The company's fear of a corporate raider, one Carl Icahn, led to a leveraged buy-out financed by replacing the pension plan with an ESOPS in 1983. The ESOPS acquired 70 per cent of the company with over a $100 million invested in Class A stock, whereas a group of managers bought the other 30 per cent in Class B shares at a cost of $4 million. These shares had doubled in value by 1987. The point is that the two classes of shares in this company conferred very different rights. Class A shares gave workers no say in the company's policy. When the company decided to go public once again, the employees did not vote on the decision, although they own 70 per cent of the shares. Further, the Class A shares have fallen in value, affecting the workers' retirement benefits (reported in *Business Week*, 26 October 1987). ESOPS are being promoted by some finance companies, notably Kelso & Co., founded by Louis Kelso, one of the leading proponents of ESOPS, to corporate management as a way of avoiding takeovers and gaining control of company stock. A company may well choose an ESOPS to raise capital in preference to issuing new shares. The reasons are obvious. Conventional share issues may dilute the voting power of the existing leadership, increasing the chances of a hostile takeover bid. Employee owners are usually well disposed to the existing management. It apparently works well. 'Employees have been extraordinarily loyal to management in takeover attempts. To get more shares in the hands of employees is an effective defensive manoeuvre, in the view of K. H. Miller, head of Mergers and Acquisitions at Merrill Lynch Capital Markets (quoted in *Business Week*, 15 April 1985, p.108). Even in these circumstances, the ESOPS still provide some benefits to employees, but give management a larger share, pegging management stock at levels 20–25 per cent above employee shares.

Somewhat belatedly, the authorities have sought to limit the use of ESOPS to prevent takeovers and to restrict the establishment of certain forms of ESOPS, where most of the benefits and the shares go to the highest paid employees in a company. But at the same time they are resisting pressures to require ESOPS to give voting rights to ESOPS shareholders.

Employee ownership has been used to obtain pay cuts or curbs when workers have bought plants which would otherwise have been closed down. This has been the case with the airline industry, in which wage agreements have allowed for a loss of pay in return for the acquisition of shares. Employees purchased 13 per cent of Pan Am, 25 per cent of Eastern and 32 per cent of Western Airlines. Only time will tell whether the value of the shares will exceed the income lost. On the other hand, collective bargaining through the trade unions has enabled workers to put representatives on the Board of Eastern Airlines. At the annual meeting of Pan Am in May 1984, employees' representatives used the voting power of their block of shares to stop a company reorganization, in the belief that the proposed new company structure would enable it to set up a new non-union subsidiary as other airlines had done. On the other hand, they could be encouraged by the 1985 study by the National Center for Employee Ownership, based on the performance of 147 ESOPS, which projected that an employee earning the median wage of $18,000 in 1983 could expect to accumulate an ESOPS share worth $31,000 in ten years and $120,000 in twenty. The first figure exceeds the net worth of half of all American families; the second exceeds the net worth of all but the top fifth.

In other cases the company has sold off a subsidiary to its employees and then continued to do business with its former employees on advantageous terms. This happened in the case of General Motors' sale of the Hyatt Clark plant in 1981. The workers agreed to a 30 per cent wage cut and to redundancies when the plant was modernized. Ford workers in Sheffield, Alabama, refused a similar deal. Becoming independent contractors means that the company does not have to pay social security or workers' compensation or into pension schemes, so it can mean a considerable saving for the companies concerned.

Any scheme proposed in the United Kingdom would differ from those developed in the United States in that the UK statutory framework would require a fair distribution of benefits without any additional benefits for management; pension funds could not be used and employees would have voting rights in the scheme's decision-making process. Many American schemes leave control with the trustees until the company loan used to purchase the shares has been paid off. These safeguards would ensure that ownership is linked with control by giving each employee member a vote. Research carried out in America indicates that employee ownership through ESOPS strengthens organizational commitment, whereas participation increases motivation and identification.

The psychological results imply that employees in employee owned companies will be more highly motivated and will more strongly identify with company goals than employees in conventional companies only if ESOPS involves participation rights for employees ... and that the productivity advantage will be strongest when employees participate in decision making. (M. A. Conte 'Participation and performance', *Society*, March/April 1986)

UK ESOPS would operate at the level of a company employing worker members. Linking ownership and control together in these ways both fulfils the aim of greater industrial democracy and makes it more likely that the benefits others have seen in terms of increased productivity and profitability in ESOPS companies do in fact materialize. ESOPS in the United States vary a great deal, with obvious abuses which would have to be carefully avoided in any more widespread application of this model in this country. What form should be adopted will be considered in the last chapter.

Chapter 5
Employee Investment Funds

The Swedish wage-earner funds are important in any debate about the role of common ownership. These aim to share excess profits as a form of postponed income, since the tax on excess profits is paid into the state pension fund. The purpose is both to achieve a greater fairness in the distribution of wealth and at the same time to strengthen Swedish wages policy and thus manage the economy more efficiently.

The funds were set up by the Social Democratic Government, which introduced legislation in 1984 to set up five regional investment funds, each with a majority (five out of nine) of union representatives on their Boards of Management. The funds are provided by profit-sharing and by a small increase in all employers' contributions to the State AIP pension system of 0.2 per cent of their total pay bills.

More precisely, profit-sharing takes the form of a tax on real profits. It amounts to 20 per cent of the profits base as defined annually, above the exemption limit. The company concerned can choose whether to regard the first 500,000 kronor or an amount equivalent to 6 per cent of its pay bill as the tax free sum. This is designed to exempt small businesses and labour intensive companies with small profits. In Sweden that meant on average that 69,700 companies out of the country's 73,000 companies would be automatically limited from the new profit tax each year. The range of companies due to pay the tax includes limited companies, incorporated societies, savings banks and mutual property insurance companies. The tax only applies to Swedish companies, including foreign-owned Swedish companies, such as Svenska Shell or Svenska IMB. The remaining companies have been paying the new tax. In assessing liability for the profits tax, the Government allows for inflation, deductions from the profits base for income tax and allocations to corporate funds.

The employee investment funds will build up until 1990, by which time the Government expects that the fund system will be fully developed. They will remain in existence and administer their shareholdings after 1990, but no new capital will be paid into them.

The employee investment funds came about as the result of a long debate within the Swedish Democratic Party and the trade union movement. The LO, the equivalent to the TUC, initiated the debate in 1975, when *Wage Earner Funds* was published. Its authors were Rudolph Meidner in conjunction with Anna Hedborg and Gunner Fond. The aims were the equalization of the difference in the structure of wealth and increased wage-earner influence over the industrial life through ownership of capital. At the same time they should constitute a complement to the "solidaric" wage policy that tends to favour profitable companies and their owners.' The aim is in fact to control, influence company policy and presumably the overall economic policy without nationalization.

Meidner's ideas were studied in the LO in the months that followed. A report, which came out in the spring of 1976, was adopted at the conference in June of that year. The main objectives were then described as counteracting the concentration of wealth, which occurs when industry finances itself, and to increase the wage-earners' influence over the economic process (see *Employee Investment Funds: An Approach to Collective Capital Formation*, Oxford, 1978). A joint report published by the LO and the Social Democratic Party added another aim – to contribute to the collective savings and capital formation for productive investments. All four aims were accepted by the Social Democratic Party in the autumn of that year.

A later contribution, *The Labour Movement and the Employee Investment Funds*, published by the LO in 1982, stated that the 'theme which runs through the proposals ... [is] that the employee influence over questions which are decisive for their own future calls for the exercise of control over capital as well as other factors' (p. 2). It also takes into account the fact that successful wages policy in Sweden led to firms being able to accumulate very large profits, which were allocated to shareholders or used to attract skilled workers by paying wages above the standard rates, contrary to the 'solidaric' wages policy.

The following principles were further worked out in a series of congresses: the funds should strengthen (a) the possibility of wages policy based on solidarity; (b) act as a countervailing force to the concentration of assets, and thus of power arising from industry's self-financing; and (c) strengthen employee influence through co-ownership.

These were the principles worked out at the 1976 LO conference and elaborated and adopted by the 1978 conference of the Swedish Democratic Party. Later it was decided that the funds should be linked to the payment of the Swedish state earnings related pension scheme, an extra resource for pensions for which Sweden foresees difficulties in meeting the commitments in the future.

The matter did not rest there. Argument about the wage-earner funds continued in LO and Party conferences until the details were finally settled. Outside the Labour movement, the funds were equally controversial. Conservative opponents described the funds in exactly the same way as they would be described in Britain if the British Labour Party had such an election commitment, as East European socialism and as a dangerous concentration of union power. They were an election issue to some extent in 1976 and again in 1979, and may have contributed to the election defeat:

The impetus for the funds came from the trade unions. The endless debate of the 1970s was described by one senior trade union official in these words:

> Palme was opposed to endorsing the thing and kept saying we need more studies. The driving force behind the whole wage earner fund debate came from the union side, and not just from LO central headquarters, but from the local network of union officials. Every time a company got into trouble and there was talk of restructuring the industry, there was also the feeling down there that if we just had wage earner funds, all this could have been avoided. The local trade union chairman would be interviewed on TV and typically gave that line. The party organisation, the mass of people in local government were at best a silent majority. They were afraid of the Meidner system because it had caused troubles in 1976, and they wanted the good old familiar social issues. (Quoted in H. Heclo and H. Madsen, *Policy and Politics in Sweden*, p. 273)

But agreement was finally reached and, with a clearer and more definite commitment to the funds and more support within the Party and the Labour movement, the social democrats won the 1982 election. Hesitancy on the part of the leadership of the Social Democratic Party in the 1970s, especially over the Meidner report and its emphasis on the funds as a means of redistributing social power delayed, their public acceptance. The Party preferred to talk about the funds as a means of providing increased capital resources for the future growth of the economy, a claim the Meidner Report did not actually make.

The funds were finally set up, and 'there is no escaping the fact that a predominantly negative or neutral Swedish public got what the union activists wanted: a system of collectivist, capital owning funds controlled by the workers' unions and derived from profits' (ibid., p. 285). The Conservative opposition, threatened to unscramble the funds but this seems less and less likely as time goes on, and the problems of re-assigning ownership rights from the collectively pooled accounts grow.

The purpose of the scheme is to invest in the risk capital market, mainly by buying shares and providing risk capital for co-operatives. The funds invest in manufacturing and related sectors, but are not allowed to buy shares in foreign companies. Share acquisitions should preferably be long-term, but short-term buying and selling is permitted when necessary. The aim is to benefit Swedish products and employment.

The funds do not, of course, have to invest, if they do not consider there are any suitable opportunities. Unused investment capital can be carried over until the following year. But once capital has been invested, a real return of at least 3 per cent must be achieved, so that the funds send 3 per cent of the capital they have invested during the year to the National Pension Insurance Fund.

The funds cannot hold 8 per cent or more of the voting rights carried by shares in a listed company. The investment funds could theoretically hold 40 per cent of a company's shares. The fourth Pension Fund Management Board could hold 50 per cent of the shares, but no more, otherwise they would be responsible for the day-to-day running of the firm, which certainly was not the Government's intention.

The funds are set up on a regional basis but are not supposed to engage in regional development in any way. The regions are roughly defined, northern, eastern and so on, and Board members are expected to live there or to be in some way connected with the region. The aim was to ensure the decentralization of the funds.

This strategy was introduced against a background of an industry dominated by large companies, mainly in private ownership. Only about 8 per cent is state owned, and 5 per cent is co-operatively owned. As in the United Kingdom, investment trusts, pension funds, insurance companies and other financial institutions predominantly own industry. Households' ownership of shares fell from 50 per cent to 30 per cent between 1975 and 1981 and probably fell to 25 per cent in 1982. Half of all households own no shares at all. Those who own the most shares own about 75 per cent of all household shares.

The LO does not make exaggerated claims for the funds. 'We are aware that [they]...will not fulfil all our ambitions for economic democracy. Many measures will be needed together with continual efforts on the part of the labour movement before we get that far – but employee investment funds are a step on the way' (*Employee Investment Funds in Sweden in 1984*, p. 15). The trade unions there rejected profit-sharing in favour of the funds. Profit-sharing was regarded as divisive between workers in profitable companies and those who were not. The funds avoided the serious conflict which would arise in the profit-sharing schemes, between the worker's role as a wage-earner union member and as a profit-orientated company person. The investment funds do not involve the wage-earner in such conflicts.

The funds have so far easily met the targets laid down, as the following figures show:

                    million kronor
       1984........1523.7
       1985........1231.0
       1986........2709.6
       1987........5464.3

       Real return

       1984–6......42 per cent
       1984–7......32 per cent (source: Swedish Embassy)

The funds now own 1.7 per cent of the share stock.

They are designed to provide investment and employment opportunities by making investment capital available to small companies through the purchase of shares, and also venture capital. So far the funds have devoted 3–4 per cent to this sector, with the eventual aim of making 6–7 per cent available for venture capital.

Acceptance by industry was slow to begin with. In the first year there was some evidence that companies tried to avoid the profits levy by the purchase of stocks, but that process could not continue. Swedish companies have gradually learned to live with the funds, and there is no evidence of foreign companies failing to invest in, or withdrawing investment from Sweden for that reason.

The funds have trade union members on their Management Boards, which is perhaps more easily accepted there given the high levels of trade union membership. The rate per employee in Sweden was 85 per cent in 1980, compared with 54 per cent in the United Kingdom and 33 per cent in West Germany. But this is not the only reason. Political education in the trade unions and the Social Democratic Party is well-organized and effective. The need for the funds was well understood throughout the whole trade union movement, and, indeed, as we have seen, the pressure for them came from the LO and its membership. And when trade union representatives are elected to the Boards, they already have relevant experience.

Opportunities for further training exist within both the blue-collar and white-collar unions. Any attempt to introduce similar funds in the United Kingdom would have to be accompanied first by a raising of the general standards of education and training for the work-force as a whole, and special training for the representatives on the Boards as well.

Sweden's economy and the funds

It is worth noting that Sweden's economy is similar in certain important respects to other Western industrial economies, including the United Kingdom's. It has become increasingly tied to global markets, with over 40 per cent of its domestic industrial production going into foreign markets in 1979. Overseas capital investment by Swedish companies has increased at a rate far in excess of the domestic rate of increase, further internationalizing the economy and making it susceptible to global conditions. It is also more exposed than most, because 'it is one of the few countries whose companies invest more abroad than foreign companies invest domestically' (K. A. Larson, 'The international dependence of the Swedish economy', in John Fry (ed.), *The Limits of the Welfare State*, London, p. 94).

Sweden, of course, had the advantage of not having to rebuild its industrial base after World War II. Industrial expansion and modernization took place during and after the war. Employment protection legislation, the Government's continued commitment to full employment, and the LO's policies of wage solidarity all helped to make the work-force more willing to accept technological change. But Sweden was badly hit by the oil shocks, and since the 1970s there has been increased concern about unemployment, capital shifts abroad and the lack of capital formation at home.

All this lay behind the push for wage-earner funds in the 1970s. Swedish labour has supported increased productivity through technological change, but has pushed for greater economic control over investments and production. 'It is simply not possible to demand that union members show moderation in wage demands if the members cannot be certain that the resources they abstain from receiving do indeed go into productive investments in Sweden, and give them sufficient influence in economic decision-making to guarantee this' (G. Fredrikson, 'Swedish social democracy at the crossroads', *Political Life in Sweden*, Swedish Information Service, New York, Oct. 1980). Put like this the funds seem entirely rational, but it is unlikely that many British industrialists would agree.

Sweden has faced significant structural problems over recent years. There have been huge job losses in timber and wood products, steel and shipbuilding. It is extremely dependent on imported oil, and was therefore badly hit by the second oil shock in 1979. When the Social Democratic Party took over in 1982, it faced a falling rate of profit, a declining level of capital investment and rising unemployment in the manufacturing sector.

Sweden's way of tackling these problems was not more public ownership, still less the attempt to use unemployment as a way of disciplining the work-force to accept lower levels of pay, or to limit the powers of the trade union movement so that workers were more prepared to accept managerial decisions. Instead, through the investment funds, it has given workers some influence over the development of capital, as well as restoring the general commitment to full employment.

Since Sweden went through the phase of being the 'sick man of Europe, with sluggish economic growth and a yawning current-account deficit' in the 1970s, its 'economic scorecard', as the *Economist* put it on 7 March 1987, 'makes impressive reading' – an unemployment rate of 2.7 per cent, an inflation rate of 3.3 per cent, one of the highest living standards in Europe and a comfortable surplus on its current account of its balance of payments, all much more successful than in the United Kingdom.

What Sweden has done is to use the 'capitalist engine to maximize output, and its public sector to redistribute the wealth thus created through taxes and transfers'. The Government's task is to help displaced workers find work in expanding industries rather than prop up declining industries. That policy seems to have worked. Export-led growth has boosted company profits to their highest levels since the 1960s and the current account is back in surplus after years in the red. The investment funds will also play their part in raising the level of capital investment of industry and provide for future welfare payments in the form of pensions. This approach to industrial policy, with industrial democracy and sharing the profits with the workers, and reinvested profits could serve us well here too.

Chapter 6
The Histradut and Hevrat
Ha'ovdim of Israel

The Histradut was founded in 1920 as the Federation of Jewish Labour with only 4,500 members and now has over a million members. It is best understood as a rough equivalent of the TUC. From the start the Histradut was not only seen as a means of protecting the interests of the workers, but also as a means under the British mandate in Palestine of developing a modern Jewish socialist state, and of providing jobs for the Jews who flocked there. It set up a variety of economic enterprises, some in the form of autonomous co-operative societies, the kibbutz and the moshavim, small-holders' co-operative settlements. It was the product of a unique set of conditions prevailing in Palestine under the British mandate. The World Zionist Organization gave only limited funds for the economic expansion of Palestine. Up to 1948, Jews who settled there had very little money of their own, and were not in a position to borrow any. Investment could come only from the profits earned in their business activities. This is the way in which the Histradut grew and developed. Capital accumulation assumed an overriding importance, but it did provide the workers with a rising standard of living.

The 'labour economy' as it is called is run by the Hevrat Ha'ovdim, the Histradut's holding company, which was founded in 1923. It comprises about 25 per cent of the national economy, mainly through six conglomerates. Koor is the largest industrial complex, employing about 34,000 workers, and Sollel Boneh is the largest construction company in the country, employing 14,000 workers at its peak. These two companies are indeed successful, but Sollel Boneh in particular was not immune from the financial difficulties facing all of Israel's construction companies during the economic crisis of the 1980s.

The Hevrat Ha'ovdim includes production, service and consumer co-operatives, a number of joint enterprises with the Government, financial institutions, such as Bank Hapo'alim, the second largest bank in Israel, and Hasneh, Israel's largest insurance company. The

Bank Hapo'alim was set up in November 1921 with a mere 2,000 Egyptian pounds, the official currency in Palestine at the time, and high hopes of selling its shares in Palestine and abroad, especially through the Zionist Movement in America. The goals of the Bank were described in terms of the Labour movement at the time: 'to assist, adopt, further and grant financial or any other assistance to all branches of activity of the institutions, federations or groups organised by the workers for the purpose of improving the conditions of their members in accordance with co-operative principles'. The Bank did not entirely serve the interests of the trade unions, especially during its period of growth in the twenties and thirties, and they had to turn elsewhere for funds. The Bank is no longer tied to the trade union movement in providing services exclusively for them. It offers a wide range of financial services to individual customers, and, although it is the largest source of credit for industry, it lends to the state and private sector as well as the Histradut. In fact, the Bank has always been 'set aside', with financial soundness being given absolute priority.

Together with the kibbutz and moshavim, the labour economy is responsible for about 75 per cent of the country's agricultural production and 20 per cent of its industrial production. About 20 per cent of employees in industrial production work in enterprises which belong to the Histradut, and its share of value-added and industrial production is a little higher than that, indicating a comparatively high capital intensity. It contributes about a quarter of the country's exports of manufactured goods. All of these indicators suggest that the Histradut enterprises are being run quite efficiently.

The holding companies, the Koor Manufacturing Group and Solleh Boneh, hold the equity, and therefore legally own the subsidiary firms involved in the production process. They run most of the research and development for the groups and are responsible for major investment funding. In the 1980s, because of the high inflation rates in Israel, they have acted as a clearing house for short-run financial operations. Since the holding company is responsible for the survival of the group as a whole, it can and does allow some of the ventures to lose money, at least in the short term. The size and variety of the Hevrat Ha'ovdim enterprises both enable them to take such risks and reduce the costs of such risks. But it is not, of course, common practice, but is in line with its commitment to 'ploughing back' profits into the enterprises. Internal financing is the accepted role for the distribution of holding companies and their subsidiaries' profits.

Projects may be accepted even if they have a lower rate of return than alternatives; some subsidiaries have been allowed to make losses for long periods of time in order to achieve social goals, such as regional development and the provision of jobs, risky ventures into new products or applying innovative technologies. Some of these have had to be scrapped, but it does allow scope for experiment. Overall, though, the holding companies have to be profitable in order to obtain credits and to tap the bond markets.

The non-negotiable shares of the holding company are distributed equally amongst all the members of the Histradut. It holds all the property rights of the Histradut enterprises, but is not directly involved in running all these enterprises. This has been devolved to groups of companies such as the Koor Group, whose hundred firms employ about 9 per cent of the workers in manufacturing industry, especially metal processing, electronics and to a lesser extent food processing and textiles. The holding companies are responsible for research and development, development finance and marketing.

The Histradut owns all these companies, but does not act directly as employer. Since the ownership rights are vested in the Histradut, the possibilities of direct worker ownership and control at enterprise level are very limited. The workers employed in Koor and Sollel Boneh are wage-earners so the immediate day-to-day situation is an employer-employee relationship based on a conventional, though modified, wage-nexus.

But there is some participation in decision-making. Industrial democracy was established as part of the Histradut enterprises from the start. However, unlike the Mondragon co-operatives, for example, prospective workers are not screened for their commitment to Histradut ideals or for working in this set-up. Worker representatives are members of the Board of Directors, but the most important democratic element is the workers' committee. The committees have a veto on dismissing workers, propose promotions and review the annual promotions list. In the last analysis, the committee has the right to appeal to the Secretary-General of the Histradut against management decisions concerning employment. Members of these committees stand a good chance of promotion, since the committee may recommend them. They can help to break down the class and occupational gaps between management and workers. Many of the present industrial leaders of the Histradut manufacturing sector started their working lives as production line operatives. The relationship between employee and management, though similar to that of private firms, is more of a co-partnership between the workers' representatives and management.

The Histradut industries pursue a generous pay-and-tenure policy. Tenure is acquired after one year's employment, which does impose higher labour costs. This is counterbalanced, according to Histradut theory, by a stronger identification with the firm. The profits of the Histradut industries go back to the trade union movement as a whole, rather than to private hands, and to the individual workers through profit-sharing schemes. This provides, it is thought, the motivation which increases productivity so that Koor and Sollel Boneh can compete successfully with private companies.

The truth of this claim has been tested and the results published in a paper in 1985 by Avner Ben-Ner and Dr Saul Estrin ('What happens when unions run firms?', Centre for Labour Economics, London School of Economics Discussion Paper No. 271, April 1985). They took a sample of fourteen Israeli industries in the manufacturing sector for ten years from 1969 to 1981. Out of the sample, Koor firms produced on average 21.8 per cent of the total value-added, using some 16.6 per cent of total employment and 24.2 per cent of total capital. The remainder was accounted for by the capitalist firms, practically all of them being unionized and bargaining with the Histradut. The capital-labour ratio was higher than for the capitalist firms and real wages were 35 per cent higher than in capitalist organizations. In spite of this the Koor firms maintained 8 per cent higher capital productivity and 37 per cent higher labour productivity than the other firms in the sample.

Other valuable data resulted from Ben-Ner and Estrin's econometric analysis. Koor firms pay higher wages not because, as might be expected, workers use their greater power to appropriate a larger share of the residual surplus, but because

> union-run firms have greater combined productivity and therefore a larger distributable surplus. In fact we cannot disinguish any significant effect from union ownership on the stress attached to profits, wages and employment ... Union power ... results in super-employment. Union run firms will contribute more to employment than capitalist-firms because productivity augmentation raises employment. Second, the presence of the union in industry in employment does not prevent fluctuations in employment ... [but] successive improvements in the market conditions in the market faced by an industry will tend to be manifested in increases in both employment and wages because the contract curve in both types of firms is positively sloped ... This may reinforce the claim by the union in Israel that it represents employed as well as unemployed workers. (pp. 24–5)

The Histradut ideal is direct control by means of union ownership of some of the 'commanding heights' of the system. It allows the trade unions to put into effect their programme of full employment, training and education and the revitalization of underdeveloped regions. The Histradut acts independently of the Government, though given Israel's history, relationships have been very close, especially when a Labour Government is in power. For a long time, for example, the Secretary-General of the Histradut, though not a member of the Cabinet, was a member of the Havereinu ('our comrades'), the small committee of the decision-makers in the Government and the state. Public clashes were rare, but they did occur, notably in the early 1970s between the Histradut and the then Minister of Finance. The Histradut has always been consulted, and was even a partner in the stabilization plans introduced by the Government in 1984 and again in 1985, to bring down inflation and reduce the balance of payments deficit. It is currently a partner in the second stage of the 1985 plan, introduced in January 1987 to maintain stability and growth. This has been one of the most difficult periods for the Histradut, since a number of its enterprises have been in financial difficulties, and contradictions have arisen in its role as a trade union and as a manager, especially in 1986. Some argue, notably Ephraim Kleiman, an economist at the Hebrew University of Jerusalem, that the Histradut enterprises ought to have aimed at the following goals:

- Provision of financial resources to the Histradut, earmarked for its general activities, or for specific activities which enhance the welfare of its membership in general.
- Action against monopolies and cartels in order to reduce prices and raise the quality of consumer goods, thus raising the real value of wages.
- Adoption of a wage policy which would compel the private sector to follow suit and increase labour's remuneration.
- Introduction of technically and managerially innovative production processes to reduce the alienation associated with most modern modes of production.
- Financial and organisational support for political parties representing the working class. (E. Kleiman, *Jerusalem Quarterly*, Winter 1987, p. 84)

It is, however, clear from the evidence cited already that the Histradut enterprises have attempted to fulfil some of the aims outlined above. But there are dangers of neglecting the consumer interests if the organization is concerned primarily and directly with the interests of the producers, as in this case with the double interest as manufacturers and representatives of union concerns. Kleiman rejects the view that the Histradut has served any of the objectives outlined above, not all of which have been accepted by it. 'It has not been a source of financial resources for the Histradut; it has not stood up to monopolies and other restrictive practices; has not provided leadership in the labour market; and has not brought any changes in the social organisation of production' (ibid., p. 89).

The Histradut has set higher standards for its workers in terms of wages and conditions of work, encouraged worker participation, if not along radical lines, and achieved higher levels of productivity and profitability than comparable conventional firms. These are important achievements, even if more could be done. It is enough to make this approach worthy of consideration for the British trade union movement.

Union-run enterprises here would, like the Histradut, be faced with a conflict between their role as employers and as representatives of workers. No magic resolution of this contradiction has been found in Israel. Risking these problems would be worthwhile for the unions for the opportunities it would provide for experiments in industrial democracy, for the jobs it would create and for the resultant economic muscle and credibility if the enterprises were as successful as the Histradut enterprises as a whole have been. It is a path the unions could take, in a positive and constructive fashion, without waiting for the election of a Labour Government.

Chapter 7
Social Ownership – Where Next?

In the first chapter of this book, the extent of the privatization programme in the first eight years of the Conservative Government was outlined. By the time of the next election in 1991 or 1992, it is extremely probable that all the basic utilities, including electricity and water, will be in private hands, together with coal, steel and other vital national industries already sold off. The costs of re-nationalizing these industries, in terms of public expenditure and legislative time, would be immense. Individual share ownership now stands at 20 per cent. Despite claims that the increase in share ownership would redistribute wealth, it certainly has not done so; in fact, the Inland Revenue's own statistics show that a wider distribution of wealth has been halted, if not reversed, since 1980.

Throughout the de-nationalization programme there has been no mention of sharing power with employees or effort to extend industrial democracy. The Government, by restricting trade union rights over the past eight years, has by its own example, by the encouragement given to the heads of nationalized industries to adopt a ruthless and abrasive style of management, endorsed the 'management's right to manage' in every possible way. Authoritarian styles of management plainly meet with the Government's approval. It is, after all, the Prime Minister's own style.

The changes brought about by the Thatcher Governments may be more apparent than real, but in the eyes of the public they are significant. The public have been given the chance of personal ownership, both of shares and houses, which many have not had before. It undoubtedly influenced voter behaviour, particularly in the south. People did think they were likely to be penalized by the transfer of utilities into public ownership. The plan to convert shares into income or capital-bearing bonds, though feasible, was quite impossible to explain on the doorstep. The fact that the Labour Party, understandably enough, did not fix a price did nothing to allay suspicions that the shares, which many felt proud of holding, would be taken away from them.

It is time to set aside regrets for the passing of state ownership of industry. The privatization programme should be welcomed in one sense and in one sense only. It has cleared the decks. We can begin again. We should certainly ignore the view of some elements in the Labour Party that anything Mrs Thatcher's Government has done should be undone. It smacks of the worst kind of conservatism. Those who strike such attitudes are guilty of a fundamental confusion, of principles with particular policies. Our principles should not change. Policies must. They are designed to apply principles in a practical way to the situation of the time. For far too long, socialist thought has been dominated by one form of social ownership. Clause 4, which encapsulates various strands of the late nineteenth- and early twentieth-century socialist thought, does stress the purpose of social ownership. The words 'common ownership' left open the question of its form.

Labour, though, has failed to consider, still less to answer, the question, did state ownership fulfil the ideals and objectives the Party rightly set for itself in Clause 4? Can even remodelled and re-vitalized state-owned industries achieve these ends? The record, even with the limited moves towards industrial democracy in the 1970s, the push towards greater efficiency and the belated recognition of the needs and interests of consumers, does not inspire confidence. It is time to move on, to look to well-tried models in other countries with more experience of socialist democracy than we have here, and to adapt and extend these models to our own economy.

We should start again by considering what Clause 4 actually says: 'To secure for the workers by hand or brain the full fruits of their industry and the most equitable distribution thereof that may be possible on the basis of the common ownership of the means of production, distribution and exchange and the best obtainable system of popular administration and control of each industry or service.' 'Common ownership' is not, of course, identical with state ownership. That is just one form, and other forms are possible. They have the advantage of extending some form of ownership to all employees, not just exchanging the private employer for the state for the favoured minority of employees.

Other aspects of Clause 4 have been effectively neglected by the Labour Party both in and out of government: 'securing for the workers ... the full fruits of their labour and the most equitable distribution thereof'. Employee share ownership schemes and the Swedish-style employee investment funds can play an important part in this process. They would be, of course, only a part of the process of achieving a more equal distribution of wealth and income. Taxation and what used to be called the 'social wage' are an essential part, provided only that we are prepared to overhaul the tax system.

Sidney Webb wisely included the words 'the best obtainable system of popular administration and control of each industry or service. He meant it only as a sop to the syndicalists, whose views he despised. But they are there, and unfortunately socialists have given too little attention to this part of the constitution. The word 'popular' has two senses, the familiar one of being liked or admired by the people, and that of being 'carried on by the people'. We should take care that the form of administration we propose for each industry and service is both appropriate and popular in both senses.

The models outlined in the previous chapters can be adapted and developed to fulfil these purposes here in the United Kingdom. They have the advanatge of keying in with the beliefs the majority now hold. The British Social Attitudes Survey 1987 shows that 80 per cent now believe that industry should share more of its profits with its employees. In fact, their views on industry in general coincide with much of what Labour has said in the past. Labour should be able to capitalize on this more than it does. More of this later.

Social ownership and the individual

Employee share ownership plans could have a significant role to play in both sharing wealth and power. But the form is vital. American schemes have often made use of pension funds and left control in the hands of trustees until the full amount of the loan used to finance the share purchase has been paid off. Ownership does not necessarily imply control in many American schemes. The pitfalls of the American schemes have been well-documented and it should be possible to avoid them by suitable legislation.

The scheme must be open to all employees. Senior management must not be allowed to obtain a higher proportion of the shares than the rest of the work-force. The schemes should be open to all and the shares must carry voting rights. They would operate at company level, or, in the case of a group, the holding company employing worker members. New tax concessions, beyond those provided in the 1978 Finance Act, would encourage companies to set up schemes.

Companies and individuals could be encouraged to set up such schemes by additional tax concessions, such as a tax exemption for all the benefits received by employees from an ESOPS. Payment of dividends on ESOPS shares should be tax deductible, and assets, whilst they remain in the ESOPS, could be tax free. Unity Trust Bank plc, established by a number of trade unions working in partnership with the Co-operative Bank, has valuable experience of establishing ESOPS in the UK, notably the Roadchefs ESOPS, and stresses other advantages a company may gain by setting up an ESOPS. Apart from tax efficiency and the value of involving all employees in the enterprise, it will enable the company to raise new equity capital to fund expansion programmes or to repay existing debts and reduce gearing, or to buy out some or all of the capital from some of the existing shareholders.

The way in which Unity Trust sets up an ESOPS provides important safeguards lacking in some of the American schemes surveyed in Chapter 5. It involves a loan to a trust by a bank, secured by a legal charge on the new assets acquired by the firm with the investment and on the shares issued to it by the trust. Shares are then issued to the trust, which pays for them through the bank loan. The trust holds the shares for all employees on equal terms, and safeguards their interests; indeed, they will have their own trustee if they wish to elect one. Bonus payments produced by the new assets and dividends declared on the shares are paid to then trust, which repays the loans over the time the arrangement lasts. Employees can realize the gain on their shares on resignation or retirement at a valuation determined by a formlua laid down in the trust deed. A business plan would be agreed between the bank, employees and the company, backed up by the employees' right to vote at shareholders' meetings.

This ESOPS model could be adapted and reinforced by further conditions which would have to be met before the tax concessions were available. These could include provisions for annual meetings for employee shareholders, balloting on key issues and details of the appointment of trustees so that employees' interests were properly represented. (These and other details are usefully set out in P. Slowe and I. Snaith, *Labour and Company law: Putting Social Ownership into Practice*, Fabian Society, Labour Finance and Industry Group, Working Group Papers 1987, pp. 39 ff.)

For some socialists, this approach to social ownership is quite unacceptable. It is simply another form of welfare capitalism. In this version of socialism, ownership and control are inextricably linked. The capitalist's control of the means of production allows him to assert his control over the workers, and their only recourse is to seize the ownership of the means of production in order to exercise power. This view ignores the fact that ownership is, of course, more complicated now than it was, with the prevalence of hired managers (who have power without ownership but are also ultimately dispensable), and minority shareholders (who have a share in the ownership of a company without any say in its policy). If these complexities are ignored, then it can be argued that, since capitalists would not willingly share ownership, the purpose must be to tie the workers more closely to the profitability of the company so that they will more willingly accept whatever is necessary to promote that.

These socialists would use the evidence already outlined about the way in which some of the American ESOPS operate, stressing the fact that they have been used to promote the interests of major shareholders or senior management at the expense of the work-force, by reducing wage demands, for example, or in extreme cases, such as Hyatt Clark, by dumping over-priced redundant plant on them. In other cases, agreements to allow employees to acquire 13 per cent of the shares of Pan Am, 25 per cent of Eastern Air and 32 per cent of Western Airlines have been at the price of generous concessions on the unions' part over wages. In practice, it is often difficult to distinguish between the uses of worker ownership as a source of capital and its use as a strategy of control.

The reasons given for ESOPS by one of the main proponents of employee ownership in the United States, Senator Long, do not inspire confidence either. In 1981, for example, the last year in which he chaired the Senate Finance Committee, he argued there that employee ownership will 'help create a stronger political base for our endangered private property' system and again, that 'capitalism really needs a broader constituency. It needs more people who regard themselves as capitalists if this system is going to survive'. He is, of course, echoing the views of his mentor, Louis Kelso, author of *The Capitalist Manifesto*. State support for ESOPS in the United States may well be seen as a form of social control, as a means of damping down wage demands and ensuring a closer identity between the worker and the firm. Something of the same purpose may lie behind the privatization programme in the United Kingdom, but less effectively since employees in the privatized industries own such a tiny proportion of the shares.

But it is important to note that in 1984 American employee owners had majority shareholdings in over 1,200 firms and 10 per cent or more of the stock in a number of firms nearer the Fortune 500 in size. By virtue of substantial ownership alone, employees have a chance of establishing industrial democracy in their companies. Sometimes worker participation is more easily granted in companies threatened with closure and saved by an ESOPS. Shopfloor committees take part in production planning committees and there may be more formal consultation at Board level. For ESOPS to fulfil any socialist objectives, they must always include a sharing of power. This is much more likely to happen if the state lays down such conditions along the lines outlined above; if the shares are owned by a perpetual trust, enabling the employees to use it as a voting block; and if the unions are actively involved in supervising the establishment of the ESOPS to ensure that abuses do not take place and that a suitable structure of democratic control is established.

All the evidence from the United States suggests that productivity and profitability increase in firms with an established ESOPS, which gives employees a real say in the running of the company. These findings are especially significant in a period in which manufacturing industry has been in decline for part of the time. If these results are duplicated in this country, then ESOPS would fulfil two important but different objectives – the creation and distribution of wealth.

The advantage of ESOPS is that they involve the individual directly, whereas the Swedish employee investment funds, described in Chapter 5, do not. It is a weakness to which Leif Blomberg, Chairman of Metall, the Swedish metal workers' union, has pointed. The funds need some kind of connection with individual employees or else his members will never understand what the funds are all about. The connection indeed is somewhat tenuous, since the funds' profits go to the pension scheme and the individual receives a better pension than he or she might otherwise have done. They were difficult to set up and Swedish employers organized huge demonstrations against them that have taken place in the major towns on 4 October each year since they were established. The first demonstration attracted 100,000 people, but on 4 October 1987 the numbers had fallen to about 10,000. The funds are now more acceptable to both unions and employers. They are organized on a regional basis but are not designed to engage in regional development.

A capital fund modelled on the lines of the Danish 'Wage Earners' Profit and Investment Fund' proposed by the Danish trade union movement was put forward in a British Labour Party Opposition Green Paper published in 1973 that bore strong similarities to the Swedish scheme (*Capital and Equality*, Report of a Labour Party Study Group [which included Barbara Castle, Nicholas Kaldor, Neil Kinnock, Ian Mikardo and others]). The justification of the scheme was that it 'could begin to change radically the balance of economic and political power as between shareholders and workers' (p. 32). The establishment of such funds merits a careful review by UK socialists of their impact in Sweden and Denmark. A fund or funds of this kind could be complementary to ESOPS. Organized on a regional basis to a greater extent than the Swedish funds, they could play a part in regional development. They would have to be judged in terms of their ability to achieve the objectives mentioned in the Green Paper of redistributing wealth and power in ways with which individual employees can identify.

These two proposals are not designed just to promote wider share ownership for its own sake; they are only valuable in so far as they share wealth and power more equally, providing workers with a real say at their place of work. The evidence that enterprises with ESOPS and greater participation are both more profitable and more productive than conventional firms underlines the value of a socialist approach to industry. It is a contribution to creating wealth as well as redistributing it, an essential feature of our industrial policy which socialists in this country all too often appear to overlook.

Social ownership and the consumer

Of all the privatization measures the sale of the public utilities, British Telecom, British Gas and the forthcoming sale of the water and electricity supply industries cause the greatest problems for socialists. It has long been argued that these are 'natural monopolies' and that the only way to ensure equal access to these services and effective safeguards for the public interest is through public ownership. Indeed, as we have seen, the 1945 Labour Government's nationalization measures, as these applied to gas and electricity in particular, were preceded both by various committee reports recommending public ownership, which in itself superseded extensive municipal ownership in the case of gas, and the establishment of the Central Electricity Board in 1926 (60 per cent of electricity supply was under municipal control by World War II).

The Conservative Government at first denied, and then, later, accepted that these industries are 'natural monopolies', finding it more convenient to accept that they were, pretending that they could be privatized in such a way that consumers, employees and the economy as a whole would benefit. In its proposals for the electricity supply industry the Government has ostensibly returned to the view that competition is essential to promote efficiency.

The controversy surrounding these or any plans to split up the electricity supply industry underlines the difficulties in introducing competition into the natural monopolies. They exist just because a single enterprise can produce more efficiently than two or more firms, even where there is more than one product involved, as in the case of telecommunications and electricity. It would be more expensive to have more than one supplier, because the costs of production can more easily be met by one large firm. Nationalization in 1945 took the form of both ensuring that there was one single supplier and that it was publicly owned. It is the Government's task to prevent the abuse of monopoly power by overpricing, for example, and to ensure in general that such an important concern acts in the public interest.

Public ownership attempts to solve the problem of natural monopolies by providing for single firm production (often by a statutory monopoly) and by stating objectives and/or constraints for nationalized industries which imply non-monopolistic behaviour. 'Similar results could be achieved by regulation of private companies, since government control does not necessarily depend on state ownership. Nevertheless, by removing a potentially powerful interest group (private shareholders) from the scene, nationalisation does in practice facilitate state control' (John Vickers and George Yarrow, *Privatisation and the Natural Monopolies*, Public Policy Centre, 1985, pp. 6–7). This is a useful summary of the rationale underlying public ownership of the basic utilities. It did provide successive Governments with the opportunity to use their powers to regulate prices and the provision of services in the public interest. That created its own problems, as Vickers and Yarrow point out.

It was not, for example, until 1967 that any systematic criteria for pricing and investment policies were laid down by the Government, the aim being to set prices equivalent to marginal costs, taking long-run, rather than short-run costs into account. The Government also laid down the real rate of return expected on investment, with a target of 10 per cent being chosen to reflect a typical rate of return on comparable private sector investment. The guidelines were difficult to monitor, and really amounted to no more than a general demand from Government that these industries should act in the public interest. No clear and effective regulatory framework was provided.

The 1967 White Paper in which these guidelines were contained was replaced by the 1978 White Paper on nationalized industries, in which financial targets were substituted for marginal cost pricing policies. Limits were placed on the net level of debt of these industries to the Government, reflecting concern with public sector debt. The nationalized industries were also supposed to meet a target of 5 per cent real return on new investment programmes as a whole, rather than the earlier requirement for a project by project approach. But although this could be regarded as a step forward in monitoring the public utilities, the level at which the financial targets were set always had more to do with the Government's overall policy than the needs and requirements of the utility concerned in its endeavour to serve the public interest. Nationalized industry prices have been used as a means of indirect taxation by successive Governments, and investment has had more to do with the Government of the day's overall investment policy than anything else. 'Over a period of several decades, nationalised industries have been left to operate with virtually undefined objectives' (ibid., p. 10).

Public ownership, in other words, does not entail public control in the public interest. It is that failure, at least as far as consumers are concerned, which has led to the public acquiescence in privatization of the utilities.

The failure has been widely recognized, except by the Government, which was very concerned about the price at which the public utilities should be sold off, but now appears to have little interest in the quality of service provided by them. All socialists agree that, whatever happens to the ownership of British Gas, British Telecom, and so on, they must in the future be properly regulated to better serve consumers and the public interest, as well as to take account of employees' concerns, while recognizing that it may not be possible to harmonize these three elements at all times. The problem is, of course, to define these objectives and to ensure that there is an adequate system of effective regulation.

Some would argue that competition should replace regulation. One such solution offered is 'organisational decentralisation and operational franchising' (cf. J. A. Kay and Z. A. Silberston, 'The new industrial policy - privatisation and competition', *Midland Bank Review*, March 1983, p. 16). They rightly argue that the American solution for its telecommunications industry of regional operating companies for the natural monopoly of local service and competing national and international trunk networks does not provide the answer. Consumers can hardly move around the country to get a better service. Franchising, in their view, would allow companies to compete for monopoly provision of the service. Regulation would still be required to ensure that the franchising companies maintained the service properly, and to ensure an effective franchise bidding system, so competition is not enough.

Furthermore, it is hard to see how this approach could work with all the public utilities in the United Kingdom. Two further considerations are important: firstly all of these industries, but some more than others, require high levels of capital investment and of research and development, both to provide an efficient service as international standards change and to keep Britain ahead in vital areas of technology, such as telecommmunications and energy; secondly, even in low technology areas, such as contract cleaning, the contracts are being sought by ever fewer but larger firms. For the public utilities, the scope for competition is limited as far as their 'core' activities are concerned, though competition may be, and often is, possible in peripheral activities.The answer must lie in proper regulation of the public utilities. British Telecom and British Gas are regulated by OFTEL and OFGAS respectively. In the case of British Telecom, OFTEL, despite the efforts it has made to be a credible regulatory body, has a number of serious weaknesses, notable among which is the fact that it has very little power to react to changes in the telecommunications industry.

British Telecom was privatized under the terms of the 1984 Telecommunications Act, which abolished British Telecom's exclusive right to run the telecommunications system. In fact, licences have been granted to British Telecom, Mercury and Kingston-upon-Hull City Council with no other operators to be considered until 1990.

The licence gives British Telecom the right to operate its public network under certain conditions: providing rural and international services, emergency services, directory enquiries and some facilities for the disabled. It also lays down the formula for price regulation, RPI−3 per cent.

As all domestic consumers know to their cost, the formula is flexible enough, because it is related to a basket of services, to allow British Telecom to raise prices for the domestic consumer and to reduce service for business, especially for large firms. It can rebalance its charges so that the various services all show the same profitability and reduce cross-subsidy. British Telecom can also re-arrange and present its accounts so that some charges can be lowered or an operation can seem to be profitable within the price restraint formula and fight off competition in this way. Prices should be controlled for individual services. Above all, this formula, as a means of regulating British Telecom's profitability, given the pace of technological change, hardly restrains it at all. This is hardly surprising since regulation was designed with its flotation on the Stock Exchange in mind, rather than providing a decent service.

The regulatory system sets prices without reference to costs, so the quality of the service is liable to be lowered. Much of OFTEL's work has been in collecting and publicizing evidence of the lower quality of important services since privatization. British Telecom is under no obligation to collect such data itself or to provide OFTEL with such a report. Some of these unprofitable services, such as call box and emergency services, have to be provided under the present licensing arrangements, but British Telecom is under no obligation to develop these or expand them. Socially useful services of this kind must be part of a new licensing agreement with British Telecom, but with more effective enforcement. OFTEL can take British Telecom to court if it breaches its licence or look to the courts to enforce these. The Monopolies and Mergers Commission can insist on improvements to the service at OFTEL's request.

Licences themselves can only be modified by the Monopolies and Mergers Commission. OFTEL has to discover any breaches of licence conditions, and is then faced with cumbersome procedures for enforcing them. In any event, it has to rely on British Telecom for its information and, of course, British Telecom has good reason for not being open about, say, its accounting methods and the way in which the allocation of costs between network and other services is carried out. OFTEL has used publicity effectively to improve the quality of service, and has made some headway, but there is scope for much tougher regulation.

OFGAS has a similar failing, as the National Consumer Council, for example, pointed out at the time, when it declared that the 'absurdly complicated price control formula seems to allow the industry to push up prices to the limits laid down ... takes no account of the possibility that it may simultaneously push up prices and reduce standards of service, and pass on directly to the consumer the cost of the gas it buys'. In the area of disconnection and consumer service, all the industry has to do is to publish codes of practice and OFGAS 'may not be able to comment on the content' (National Consumer Council press release, 8 Jan. 1986).

So far, UK regulation leaves much to be desired. The American pattern is sometimes held up as a model, but there are certain disadvantages, especially in the field of energy supply. A single regulatory body deals with a range of utilities in the United States, as well as separate agencies at local level. Economic regulation of electricity, for example, is in the hands of the local Public Utility Commissions. Much can be learnt from the way in which these operate, and they would repay further study by the Labour Party. These have significant powers, which can work to the benefit of the consumer, but do not encourage the development of a coherent, national energy policy. Disagreements between the industry and the local Public Utility Commissions are settled by slow and costly litigation. Other problems have arisen with the American version of regulation, such as 'regulatory capture', in which the regulatory agency, initially at least, becomes identified with the interests of the firm it regulates. Regulation has usually prescribed a maximum rate of return on assets, which gives little incentive to efficiency, since it allows cost to be passed on in prices.

The present UK Government was, as we have seen, more concerned with the proceeds from privatization than with preventing the abuse of monopoly power. It gave little thought to adequate regulation. A much more effective regulatory system will have to be provided in the future, even if a Labour Government should decide to take the public utilities back into public ownership, which would take much legislative time and pre-empt some resources, and even if the shares were exchanged for bonds, as the Labour Party proposed before the 1987 election, interim 'public interest regulation' should be provided. The TUC recognized this in its document 'Industries for the People', published in 1987, and argued for the immediate implementation of regulation by an incoming Labour Government, which, in the case of British Telecom, would cover pricing, purchasing policies, research and development, high technology investment, overseas investment, industrial democracy and its public sector obligations in general.

Since it is likely to be both impractical and unpopular to re-nationalize the public utilities, far more attention must be given to regulation. The National Consumer Council proposed a single regulatory body, which would then be able to compare the advantages and disadvantages of each of the utilities and would resist the problem of being 'captured' by any single industry. In certain areas, such as energy, where most of the participants are utilities, regulation would be able to take account of strategic questions. This should be quite separate from a new service to consumers to deal effectively with their complaints, and to make representations on their behalf. American experience suggests that it is better to separate the roles of regulation from consumer protection and the fight for consumer rights. Public Utility Commissions there now hear consumer advocates arguing the case against price increases.

The regulatory body should be concerned with the public interest and debates about issues such as tariffs, levels of service, the provision of non-profit making services as publicly as possible. There will no doubt be limits to which the debate can be carried on in public, since this in itself, will make regulation much more effective. It is not intended to replace management of the industry concerned, but to monitor it, prevent abuses of monopoly power and encourage best practice. It should take account of the issues outlined by the TUC above. The regulatory body would have general duties as far as the consumer is concerned to protect their interests as regards prices, the terms of supply (especially the universality of the service provided), the continuity of supply, its quality, the efficiency and economy of the services provided and to promote competition in the areas where this is possible.

The regulatory body should be able to investigate any aspect of an industry's operations, perhaps at the request of the Government, in response to public concern over some aspect of the performance of one of the utilities.

The National Consumer Council and others have suggested that the industry's performance could be judged against the kind of criteria set out in the Price Commission Act 1977, Section 2, which required the Commission 'to have regard to all matters which appear ... to be relevant with a view to restraining charges consistent with making of adequate profits by efficient suppliers', especially:

- The need to recover costs incurred in efficiently supplying goods and services and in maintaining the value of the relevant business.
- Encouraging reductions in costs by improvements in the use of resources and of securing reductions in prices of goods and charges for services in consequence of such improvements.
- The need to earn profits which provide a return on the capital employed sufficient, taking one year with another, to defray the cost of capital (including compensation for risk); to provide money for, and to encourage the promotion of, innovations and technical improvements in and expansion in the United Kingdom of the enterprises which consist of or include the relevant businesses.
- The need to take account of changes in prices in determining the value of assets.
- Promoting competition between suppliers or, where competition cannot be promoted, by restricting prices and charges.
- The need to establish and maintain a balance between supply and demand.
- The need to avoid detriment to the UK balance of payments and the need to increase the share of UK enterprises in markets in the United Kingdom and elsewhere.
- Maintaining the quality of goods and services and satisfying the demands of users of goods and services.

Within this framework, the regulatory body can check whether the contracts between customer and industry are 'fair and reasonable' and carry out 'value for money' audits. The utilities would be obliged to carry out the Commission's recommendations – on pain of having to reduce their prices if they did not.

A tougher regulatory framework of this kind could go a long way towards removing at least the worst abuses of private monopolies providing basic services. This should be combined with part ownership by the Government of the basic utilities. Up to a 10 per cent stake would give the Government the necessary influence over investment policy and other aspects of the industry's policy. The stake would be acquired, where necessary, by purchasing the shares on the Stock Exchange or by offering, but not enforcing, the exchange of shares already owned by the public for Government securities.

It would be better to present the public with this clear-cut choice between uncontrolled private monopolies and properly regulated but still privately owned basic utilities. Privatization has forced socialists to realize that policy had stopped with the public owner-ship of the utilities, with little concern for whether or not they were serving the public interest or the consumer. Public ownership did not and will not automatically ensure that they do. Socialists would be better employed in making sure that these utilities, however owned, achieve the goals set for them.

Co-operatives

In Chapter 3, one of the most important and well-known co-operatives, Mondragon, was carefully examined to discover the reasons for its success and endurance, and if the so-called Mondragon 'experience' is unique. The conclusion is that co-operatives along the lines of Mondragon could be established elsewhere. The Mondragon co-operatives have had access to capital, or, at least, they saw the need to ensure this by providing their own bank from the start. They saw the importance of good management and have made provision for it. No one could argue that Mondragon has been less well-managed than its conventional counterparts. The complementary relation-ships between the groups of co-operatives provide each one with mutual support, and increase the chance of survival far beyond that of a small co-operative struggling alone.

These conditions can be reproduced in Britain; first by ensuring proper access to capital for the new co-operative. State funding could be made available. There are interesting historical precedents for this. Nineteenth-century French socialists such as Louis Blanc made state aid for co-operatives one of their policy demands. Karl Marx appeared at first to accept this view. Usually contemptuous of co-operatives, and of their continued existence in a capitalist world, he nevertheless said, in his inaugural address to the First International, that 'co-operative labour ought to be developed by national dimen-sions, and consequently fostered by national means'. But, by 1874, when state aid for producers' co-operatives became part of the programme for Germany's new Social Democratic Party, Marx rejected any such proposal. 'As far as the present co-operative societies are concerned, they are of value only in so far as they are independent creations of the workers and not protégés either of the government or of the bourgeois.' But if there is to be any viable alternative to private and state ownership, then some form of state support or access to sympathetic capital, such as co-operative banks should be made available.

At present, various forms of financial assistance are available for co-operatives through local authorities and the use of the enterprise allowance; and other forms have been proposed by the Labour Party, including the establishment of local co-operative development agencies, investment by local enterprise boards and the use of regional investment funds. The full range of tax concessions and current support for small businesses should be made available through Industrial Common Ownership Finance Ltd under the auspices of the Industrial Common Ownership Act 1976. But there are always dangers, quite apart from wastefulness, in the proliferation of agencies. It would be better to channel funds through one agency, acting in conjunction with a state investment bank, or, at the very least, it ought to co-ordinate the various forms of financial support. The Co-operative Development Agency is well-placed to fulfil this role, as well as to promote co-operatives and advise those who wish to set one up. It receives a derisory sum at present, and its funds and staff would have to be substantially increased.

Co-operatives should provide their own finance for investment out of retained earnings, by adopting the procedure of 'statutory indivisible reserves' on the model of the French co-operatives. Some of the profits would be placed in a fund which was owned collectively and could not be distributed to members. These profits would be free of corporation tax, deductible in the way that loan interest or money allocated to an employee profit-sharing scheme is deductible under the Finance Act 1978 provisions.

If co-operatives are to flourish, it will be necessary to reform and clarify the law under which they operate, mainly the Industrial Common Ownership Act 1976. It would be easier for co-operatives to have a specific legal structure and to face fewer restrictions in the kind of operations they can carry out. They are at present limited to carrying on an industry, business or trade. Co-operatives should be free to carry on any kind of activity, to enter into partnerships with non-co-operatives and, as a means of encouraging growth, provided they had no right to vote. This would require up-dating, and eventually replacing legislation to take account of, and improve on, recent changes in company law. (A full description of the necessary legal changes is given in P. Slowe and I. Snaith, *Labour and Company Law: Putting Social Ownership into Practice*, Labour Finance and Industry Group, Working Group Papers, 1987).

Conventional companies are already free to convert to co-operatives under the procedures laid down under the Industrial and Provident Societies Acts, and the tax concessions granted in the 1975, 1976 and 1978 Finance Acts, but few conventional companies have taken advantage of them. Exemption from corporation tax has been proposed as an additional inducement, and allowing for the existence of a special class of company, a common ownership company. Converting a company into a co-operative without share transfers means applying the basic co-operative principle of a limited return on capital and equal voting. What would happen in such a conversion is that the ordinary shares would become non-voting redeemable preference shares with partially cumulative dividends, and, second, that workers would be issued with new shares with equal voting. It would then become a common ownership company. Such proposals should be seriously considered, and perhaps taken on board by a future Labour Government. But even if they are, it seems unlikely that many large conventional companies will convert to co-operatives. The real possibility of expansion lies in the small- to medium-sized firm sector of manufacturing industry. It is quite extensive. About one-third of manufacturing production is carried out in firms with 200 employees or less, and about half in firms with 500 or less. Just over 40 per cent of employees work in firms with less than 500 employees. Five hundred or so employees is generally reckoned to be the maximum for a co-operative to work properly.

It would be important to extend the third alternative to cover as many of the employees in these firms as possible. It would be another way of fulfilling the twin ideals of extending industrial democracy and a more equal access to wealth. The extension could well lead to more productive and efficient enterprises, since the workers will have a greater commitment to its success. This will only happen if management training, advice and training in business and technical skills are readily available. The extension of greater industrial democracy, whether through participation or workers owning and managing their own enterprises, will not work without the proper educational background. A Labour Government pursuing these ideals would initially have to make full provision through the existing educational institutions for that.

Chapter 8
Social Ownership and the Economy

State ownership gradually came to be regarded as a means of controlling the economy, though it was not intended to be at the outset. It is perhaps understandable that this view did prevail since part of the aim of public ownership was to dispossess capitalists, an aim which became linked with the belief that capitalism would lead to the increasing impoverishment of the working classes. There even seemed to be strong justification for this view, given the economic circumstances of the 1920s and the early 1930s.

It was thought that state ownership would bring benefits to the working classes because the profits of the industry concerned would go to the public purse. At the same time these industries would not sacrifice the workers' interests to the pursuit of profit; they would serve both the interests of their employees, by providing decent conditions of employment, and the public good. These two objectives could obviously contradict each other, and much of the subsequent history of the nationalized industries has been an illustration of this. No one ever asked the question initially, under what efficiency criteria should nationalized industries operate? Nor was it adequately answered subsequently. No satisfactory decision was ever taken about the responsibility for determining these criteria – Government departments or the management? What actually happened was that power to take managerial decisions constantly oscillated between the Government and management, with the Government of the day interfering in sensitive decisions, often whilst loudly proclaiming that it was doing nothing of the sort.

Nevertheless, Labour remained committed to nationalization. By the end of the post-war Labour Governments, the Government had nationalized Cable and Wireless, coal, steel, telecommunications, the railways, gas, electricity and water, 20 per cent of the economy in all, but had begun to realize that they did not control the economy, and made no real attempt to provide themselves with the means of doing so. The Labour Party in the fifties recognized this failure, talked of the importance of capturing the 'commanding heights' of the economy, but provided no framework for the planned economy. Instead, as we have seen, the Party began to produce its shopping lists of the industries to be nationalized. Such lists, which have been produced on more than one occasion, lack any coherence. They are no substitute for any attempt to plan the economy.

But then and since, Labour's policies have been bedevilled by the assumption that control entails ownership. Repeated calls for more public ownership just do not take account of the way in which the country's economy has changed. Nationalization of multinational companies makes little sense.

Some would claim that ownership is not completely irrelevant. It does influence company behaviour. If ownership can be dismissed so lightly, then it is impossible to explain the world-wide bandwagon for privatization. The answer seems to be quite simple; it is a convenient way of transferring wealth into private hands, with the gloss that it is in the interests of efficiency or competition.

The argument seems to be that privately owned industries may be subject to the monitoring and disciplines of the market, but in an economy in which these are weak, nationalization can improve the internal efficiency of the industry concerned. But, however weak a domestic market may be, almost no industry, privately or publicly owned, can be insulated from competition and the international market. Estrin's argument does not take this point on board, but points out that the different types of ownership will affect the behaviour of firms in different ways and will set different objectives for the enterprise. What has not been shown is that state ownership is essential for efficient monitoring in a weak market or that the same objectives could not be achieved in different ways.

Owning just a few significant industries has plainly not solved the economic problems facing Britain. Any approach Labour adopts must be far more wide-ranging than just selecting a few key basic industries as candidates for re-nationalization. Other more success-ful socialist economies, such as Sweden's, with only 8 per cent of industry in state ownership, provide a more useful model. Its policies are designed to achieve a high rate of growth since employment will follow in its train. And, as we have seen, Sweden has succeeded in achieving growth, and a much lower level of unemployment than other European countries, by the policies it has pursued since the Social Democratic Party was re-elected in 1982, after seven years in opposition. At the same time, worker participation and the pursuit of equality have not been neglected.

Turning to the British economy, Labour has long recognized that its fundamental weakness lies in the manufacturing sector, which has itself been further severely damaged by the present Goverment's economic policies especially during its early years in office.

Others share this assessment. UK investment has been below the OECD average. British machinery is less technically advanced and less well maintained and utilized than in more competitive countries. (see, for example, Daly, Hitchins and Wagner, 'Productivity, machinery and skills in a sample of British and German manufacturing plants', in the *National Institute Economic Review*, February 1985). Britain's performance in business research and development expenditure has fallen behind that of our competitors in recent years, with industry's own contribution at 1 per cent being particularly low.

The Confederation of British Industry argues that the case for investing in the UK has not been strong when compared with Germany, for example, since UK productivity still lags well behind West German levels, partly because of the German insistence on training at all levels. Profitability in the UK manufacturing sector as a whole, as measured by the rate of return on assets, still seems to be much lower than in West Germany. Average pre-tax returns in manufacturing are still almost double those in the UK (17 per cent compared with 8 per cent in 1986), and average manufacturing productivity is still around twice British levels (see, for instance, G. F. Ray, 'Labour costs in manufacturing', *National Institute Economic Review*, May 1987). Manufacturing output in the UK has fallen over the last ten years by 3 per cent and risen by 16 per cent in West Germany. As a result, UK manufacturing is a much smaller share of GDP than in West Germany, 21 per cent compared with 33 per cent in 1986.

This is the Confederation of British Industry's analysis of the present state of the UK manufacturing industry in their City/ Industry Task Force's Report, *Investing for Britain's Future* (Oct. 1987). As a result of this report, they conclude that 'investment is the key', and long-term investment in particular, to a successful future for British industry. Chancellor Lawson and the Government only give a token assent to this view. The Labour Party, like the CBI, has argued the case for long-term investment in industry for the past ten years.

The present Government takes a relaxed view of manufacturing industry and its impact on the economy, despite the fact that the current balance of payments deficit was expected to reach £12bn, 2½ per cent of GDP by the end of 1988, because of the contribution both to the balance of payments and the economy generally made by

North Sea oil and invisible earnings. The deficit for 1988–9 may in fact reach £10 billion, 2¼ per cent of GDP. These two elements have served to conceal from the Government and the public alike the dangers in the accelerating decline of manufacturing industry, leading Chancellor Nigel Lawson to dismiss the contribution made by industry by claiming that Britain could afford to become a 'low-wage, low-tech' economy. Plainly, Britain cannot lower its wage levels or its unit costs sufficiently to compete with the low-cost developing countries to which multinational companies, in particular, look for cheap labour.

Does manufacturing industry matter? Again the Confederation of British Industry's analysis sounds a useful warning.

> Without domestically based world class companies, there is a danger that Britain could become a satellite economy. Already, there are too few world class British based manufacturing companies who are world leaders. Of the hundred largest non-oil industrial companies in the world (ranked by sales), only six are wholly based in Britain [eight are West German and sixteen Japanese]. (ibid., p. 11).

During the past eight years, there has been relatively little investment in new plant and equipment, so manufacturing industry is now working fairly close to full capacity, and there is little potential for Keynesian reflation, if we want both growth and full employment, then, given the gradual decline in North Sea oil, Britain's long-term economic performance must be improved. At the end of their thorough survey of Britain's de-industrialization, Rowthorn and Wells conclude,

> The key to such an improvement lies in manufacturing industry. Services can make a useful contribution, but rapid and sustained economic growth is impossible without a massive increase in manufacturing output. This in turn requires a large-scale programme of capacity-creating investment within the framework of a coherent industrial policy, whose aim is to create a dynamic and competitive manufacturing sector. (R. E. Rowthorn and J. R. Wells, *De-industrialisation and Foreign Trade*, Cambridge, 1987).

Such a programme would have the support of the public, who both favour more investment and understand the reasons for it, but do not believe that more profit automatically means more investment (*British Social Attitudes*, 1987, pp. 34–5). They might well favour policies which involved directing profits to investment.

If investment is the key, then the role of Government and its strategy should be clarified. First of all the Government must recognize the need to develop a highly competitive manufacturing sector. As we have seen, this has been the underlying weakness in the present Government's strategy. It has notoriously failed to re-invest the £60 billion North Sea oil revenue available to it between 1979 and 1987, and allowed the deficit in manufactured goods to reach £7.3 billion in 1987 and net manufacturing investment to fall below 1979 levels for each of the years between 1980 and 1987. Getting investment in manufacturing and research and development to the levels of our main competitors should be a major priority for the next Labour Government.

It will not do to encourage investment in declining industries. The policy should be the deliberate restructuring of industry over time towards higher value-added, higher productivity industries, especially in the realm of high technology. Some of these important high value-added sectors have actually declined – motor vehicles, data-processing, telecommunications and audio equipment. Britain's share of world exports in technologically intensive products fell from 10.8 per cent in 1980 to 7.6 per cent in 1984. Such a policy can provide jobs, as long as it is accompanied by a thorough programme of education and training. This has, for example, been Sweden's experience. It requires careful planning, so that the training and re-training programmes are in place as industrial restructuring is in progress. Any restructuring must be accompanied by a recognition that the workers involved should not be thrown aside on the scrap heap of unemployment, but equipped to find other jobs through retraining, with perhaps grants to help them move. Housing policy obviously has an important role to play here.

The Government should also adopt aggressive domestic and international business strategies, with the following features. Capital should be directed to targeted industries, partly through Government funding and incentives for high-tech investment. Joint funding for major development projects should be established. Government funding should be used quite deliberately to enable key industries develop, and then phased out as these become successful. Tax incentives for research and development should be made available, and soft loans to enable small- to medium-sized firms to lease new technology equipment or purchase it, so that they can produce better quality goods at competitive prices. Even if funds are available for small or high-risk ventures, the financing costs are high. Large companies in Britain have made considerable progress in applying new technology to the production and distribution of goods, but are still well behind their main competitors in Germany and Japan in particular. If the small business sector is to thrive, carefully targeted assistance must be given. This can take a variety of forms, including the use of public sector purchasing to promote long-run industrial competitiveness.

The way in which the value of a project for both Government, industry and the financial institutions is assessed should be changed. It is necessary to take a long-term view. Major projects should be evaluated for their impact on the competitive cost position and market share for the whole business over a seven-year period. Macro-economic policies should secure a cost advantage for exports, in a situation in which encouraging the domestic market through import controls is no longer open to the country.

It can be seen from this broad outline of industrial policy that little depends on state ownership of specific industries or even key companies in a particular sector. State ownership was never enough to promote investment of this kind, though the purchasing policies of state-owned industries like British Telecom had a significant part to play. Industrial policy under a Labour Government went wider than ownership.

But the strategy should be reinforced by setting up a state holding company which would take a stake of up to 10 per cent of a company's shares in a key sector in the areas the Governmemt wanted to develop, to influence its investment policy along lines which fitted in with the Government's overall approach. The holding company would operate at arm's length from Government; it would not be run by Whitehall, but would encourage industrial development in line with the Government's objectives.

Its purpose would be to assist industry with one of its most difficult tasks, managing the decline of some industries by scrapping high-cost capacity and encouraging small companies to merge and others to go for a market share by proper distribution and marketing arrangements, and competitive pricing policies, wherever possible, given, for example, European Community competition rules. Some British companies plan their investment policy in this way; others do so, but ineffectively, and the rest take a short-term view. Falling market shares in a range of manufactured goods show where the weaknesses lie.

One of the problems facing the UK is that the business community regards any Government initiatives in industrial strategy with suspicion, if not outright hostility. They consider that Government should restrict its intervention to providing suitable economic conditions – public sector investment, a competitive rate for sterling, both of which are important, and ensuring that public expenditure does not crowd out private sector investment, a somewhat old-fashioned view. Industrial policy should not be presented as a way of correcting the private sector's social and economic failures, but as a way of creating wealth, so that living standards throughout the community will rise and public services be properly funded. At the same time, the private sector must realize that more successful economies than ours – Japan and Germany, for example – plan their industrial development with Government and industry working together. Better ways must be found for the financial and the industrial sectors to work together to produce the levels of long-term investment industry will require. Labour has stressed the need for an investment bank to provide the long-term credit industry needs. This is a common feature of other successful economies. Germany has its Kreditanstalt fur Wiederaufbau (KfW), with capital provided by the Federal and Lander Governments, and Sweden its State Investment Bank, specializing in providing medium- and long-term credit at fixed interest rates in co-operation with or through a subsidiary with twenty-four regional funds.

Investment in production will not be enough unless other factors are taken into account in a company's plans, such as product design, reliability, distribution, marketing, delivery dates and after sales service. Research and development play a key role in all of this. Britain should rely on technological innovation and on quality differentials in order to gain a market share, and the chances of doing this are greater in high research intensity industries such as electronics, motor vehicles and pharmaceuticals. A recent National Economic Development Council paper stressed that improvements in non-price competitiveness, and the consequent effects on UK trade could help to create many new jobs.

The essential improvements here will not be brought about by direct Government action or intervention, but, instead, ways must be found through the tax system, loans and subsidies to make the capital available to industry. The funds should be channelled through a state investment bank in the form of loans at suitable rates of interest rather than a Government department. Real interest rates to the corporate sector in the UK have been a serious disincentive to investment over the last eight years and have been consistently higher than our main competitors'. The state holding company will encourage the right kind of development by taking a stake in companies at a particular stage, and the holding need not be permanent, or by entering into joint ventures to set up a new enterprise in a sector the Government wants to develop. Such 'intervention' by the Government may be temporary and there may be no policy intervention for long periods in some sectors. State ownership would obviously work against this kind of flexibility.

industrial policy, given the need to keep up with rapid technological change and the ability to move into new markets with some speed.

What this book demonstrates is that the next Labour Government will be able to introduce a series of measures that will promote industrial development, thus creating the wealth the country needs. The models of common ownership provided by ESOPS and co-operatives, both in Britain and elsewhere, show that the ideals of Clause 4 can be far more adequatelty fulfilled than they ever were through state ownership. Properly set up and funded, they enable employees to have a real say, not only in the day-to-day running of the enterprise but in its long-term strategy as well. Wealth and power can thus be shared in a way nationalization did not permit. The individual employee benefits and the community reaps its reward as well. All the evidence points to the greater profitability and competitiveness of the enterprises in which power is shared.

Understanding Clause 4 in this way provides a standpoint from which to criticize the Government's own privatization programme. The few shares many individuals and employees have acquired in each share flotation, and will no doubt acquire in future privatiza-tions, have not and will not share wealth and power more equally. Privatization is not, of course, intended to achieve those ends, despite the propaganda. Labour should continue to attack the Government's programme from this standpoint. City financiers will make their pile out of the share flotations, basic utilities will be privatized once again with little regard for health and safety or the consumer, and with scant consideration for the possible abuses of monopoly power.

Labour can afford to welcome the fact that the decks have been cleared. Labour cannot and should not cling, nervously and conser-vatively, to old forms devised in quite different circumstances. The 1980s and the 1990s demand a fresh approach, yet one in which Labour returns more decisively than ever before to its original ideals of 'securing for the workers by hand or by brain the full fruits of their industry and the most equitable distribution thereof' and of empowering employees at their place of work.

Index of Proper Names

Lesley M&S8

FABIAN SERIES — already published

IMPRISONED BY OUR PRISONS
by Vivien Stern

Overcrowded, mismanaged, hidden from view and ignored – who do our prisons serve, and what are they for? Do they protect society from a dangerous criminal threat? Punish those who have gone astray? Re-educate those who have – for whatever reason – fallen foul of the law? Or are they an outmoded, ineffectual and unimaginative response to a variety of social problems?

Vivien Stern unlocks the prison doors and suggests new, more humane approaches to the problems 'inside'. She examines the concerns of the men and women who live and work within them, exposing the abuses of power, the denial or rights, and the humiliation and degradation that the system imposes.

Arguing against prevalent calls for stiffer sentences, she explores the possibilities for reducing the use of custodial penalties and easing the tensions within our overpopulated prison buildings. She also demonstrates a variety of solutions from abroad that might easily be implemented here. Some would transform our prisons into infinitely more humane institutions; others are shown to have decidedly sinister implications.

This challenging and far-sighted book will cause us to re-evaluate our responsibility for our prisons, and for those we confine in them.

Vivien Stern is Director for the National Association for the Care and Resettlement of Offenders.

ISBN 004 4452977

GOODBYE COUNCIL HOUSING
by David Clapham

The public housing sector, under attack from the Government and plagued by its own shortcomings, is in a crisis which could lead to its demise. But – since 1919 – council housing has been seen as a key instrument for achieving social objectives in housing, and this crisis therefore raises crucial questions. Is council housing an effective way of achieving these objectives? What strategy should the Government's opponents pursue?

This provocative contribution to the debate over the future of council housing will stimulate discussion about social objectives in housing, and about alternatives to council housing which aim to give tenants more control over their housing situation.

David Clapham is Assistant Director of the Centre for Housing Research at the University of Glasgow. He has written extensively on council housing and housing co-operatives.

ISBN 004 4452969

FABIAN SERIES — forthcoming

COMPETITIVE SOCIALISM
Austin Mitchell

One of Labour's central problems is how to develop an economic policy which is both socialist and in tune with the new expectations of the electorate. Austin Mitchell argues that the two are entirely compatible, and that British society and socialism can be transformed by a policy of economic expansion.

Austin Mitchell is MP for Great Grimsby and an economist.

April 0 04 440431 X

FABIAN SERIES — forthcoming

CAN LABOUR WIN?
Martin Harrop and Andrew Shaw

With three electoral failures behind them, is Labour a
spent force? Martin Harrop analyses what went wrong
for Labour in 1979, 1983 and 1987, and gives a
prescription for their success at the next election.

Martin Harrop is Lecturer in Politics at the University
of Newcastle-upon-Tyne
Andrew Shaw is lecturer in Politics at the University of
Liverpool.

April 004 4404328

FABIAN SERIES — forthcoming

REFORMING WHITEHALL
Clive Ponting

A 19th century institution in the late 20th century: closed, unaccountable and inadequate. That is how Clive Ponting sees Whitehall, and few people are better qualified than he to make such comments. In *Reforming Whitehall* he describes what must happen if the system is to lose this widely held reputation and become the efficient and open machine we need.

Clive Ponting is a writer and former civil servant.

April 004 4404336